Branching Out ❧ Tree Quilts ©

by Carolann Palmer

1

Dedication

To my mother, Edith Moor, who introduced me to sewing and quilting at a very early age, and to my father, Warren, who spent many vacation hours with me, camping and hiking among beautiful trees.

And to my special husband, Eric, who supported me in this project and repeatedly stated, "You can do it."

Thanks!

Acknowledgments

A special thanks to Nancy Martin from That Patchwork Place who believed in me and pushed me along in this project.

Friends are fantastic! Quilter friends are double fantastic! A bouquet of thanks to members of the Seattle Quilt Troupe who listened, gave advice and encouragement, and then helped in the quilting of the following quilts.

Clarice Jacques -- Forest Primeval
Gayle Ducey -- The Woodland Tree
Carol Seeger and Peg Storey -- The Love Tree
Ellie Strain -- The Bear Tree
Carol Walkky -- The Alpine Tree
Two of my daughters also helped quilt:
Jan Cote -- The Wild Goose Tree
Carolee Hammer -- Forest Glorious

To Elizabeth, Ruth, and Vera go thanks for helping in the early development of the designs. We had a lot of fun!

Finally, thanks to members of Quilters Anonymous and my family for their support and words of encouragement.

Credits:
Photography. . . . . Carl Murray
Illustration and Graphics. Stephanie Benson

All quilts and patchwork projects made by the author unless otherwise noted.

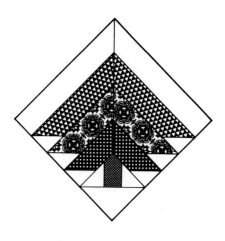

0-943574-36-6

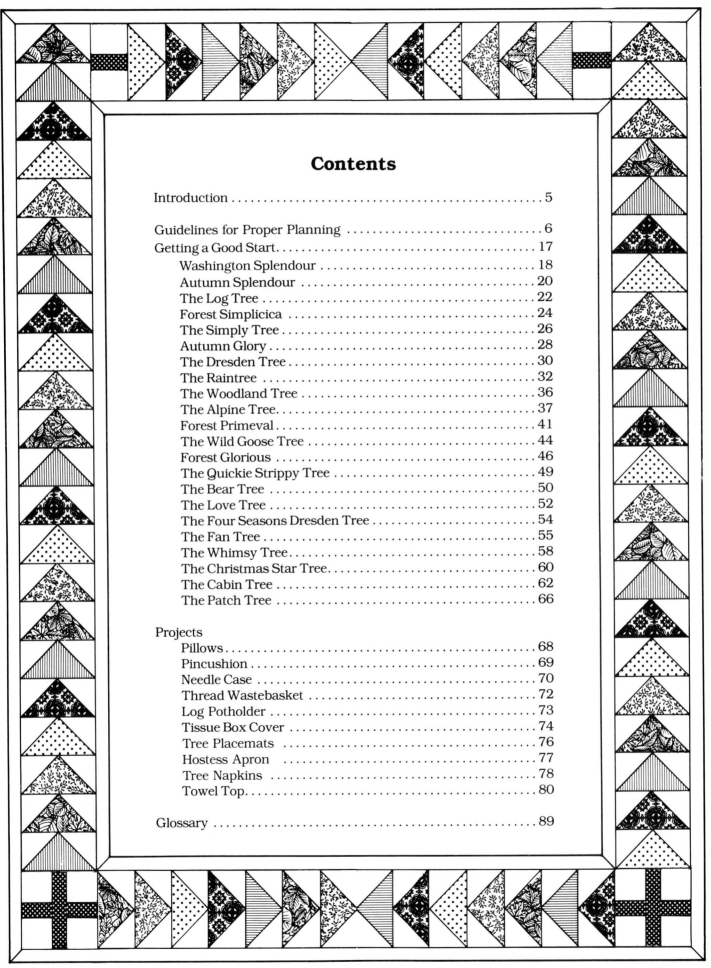

Contents

Preface

One of my earliest memories is the joy of being tall enough so the top of my head would brush the bottom of the quilt my mother was working on as it was stretched out full size in an old fashioned frame. For several weeks at a time the rest of the family had to walk around the dining room by going through the hall because the quilt, frame, and quilters occupied the entire room. I got to go under the quilt!

The first quilt I can remember is the one my mother made for me using scraps from the dresses from the first six years of my life. It is a Sunbonnet Sue. Then, I had a hard time understanding why it wasn't finished until I was twelve and she traced around my hands for the pattern in the top corners. Now, I understand that feeling perfectly!

The first of many quilts I have made was done about twenty-five years ago. I used liquid embroidery to make blocks of the state birds and flowers. It is faded now, but is still much treasured.

I have made and hand quilted over sixty quilts for babies of my friends and thoroughly enjoy seeing some of the ragged, tattered remains of them years later. Many others have hung on their nursery walls and these equally bring joy and satisfaction.

My fascination with trees has been a lifelong diversion. When I was a child, my parents took me on an annual two-week vacation and we would travel to one of the national parks and camp in the deep forest. We would hike and live among the trees. I remember those excursions as being so peaceful. As my children grew up, we would as a family go camping and have many similar pleasurable experiences.

The writing of this book was bound to happen. My first tree quilt, Washington Splendour, was an artistic experience for me. I entered it in a Tree in Art exhibit and won a prize. It was this event that spurred me on.

Thinking of how many ways to depict a tree in a quilt has been in my thoughts these past months and here are the results. Some traditional quilt patterns have been used. The round and triangular shapes especially lend themselves to becoming trees. I hope you will use these patterns, rearranging and adding your own variations. Have fun!

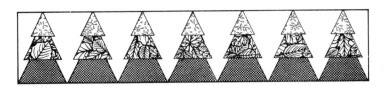

Introduction

Branching Out: Tree Quilts contains directions for twenty-two quilts and ten projects. The quilts are in varying sizes and most can be made larger or smaller according to your needs. The projects are practical and decorative and cover a variety of items.

There are four sections in this book. Section 1 is designed to give helpful guidelines for planning your quilt or project. You may choose to use these patterns as is or for a springboard to something different.

Section 2 contains the tree quilt directions, including templates, photographs, and helpful suggestions. The projects in section 3 give ideas for using single blocks in home decorating, clothing, or making sewing aids like a pincushion or needle case.

Section 4 gives details on finishing a quilt top once it is sewn together, and defines some techniques used in the text. If you are new to quilting, this section will guide you to completion of your project. If you are an experienced quilter, you may prefer to use your own methods.

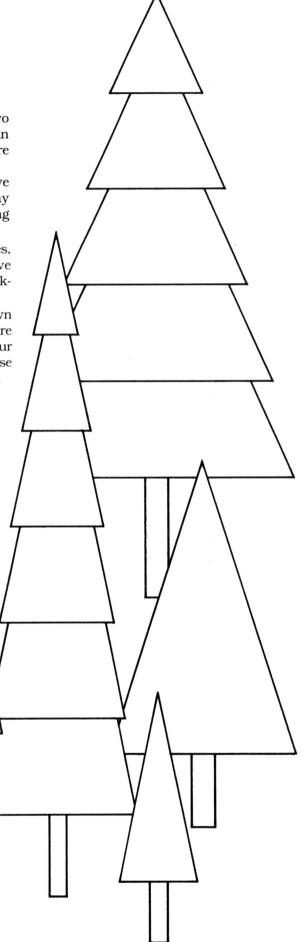

Guidelines for Proper Planning

Fabric Selection

One look in a fabric store will show you the many choices available today. Certainly, 100% cotton is the easiest with which to work and the prints available are myriad. There are many fabric families that have been manufactured with the quilter in mind. It is a real treasure to find four or five prints and solids that are the same color and are compatible with each other.

Be sure to preshrink your fabric before use. Wash until the water is clear. This is best done in a wash basin in your sink so you can see the color of the water. Do not use bleach in this process, as it may cause the fabric to change color.

Color

Color is one of the most important design elements in a quilt. Have you noticed how different quilts can be when all are made from the same pattern, yet have different colors? The pattern and overall effect changes dramatically with each quilt.

Be sure to have a variety of print sizes in your selection. Include large prints, tiny calicoes, stripes, and dots along with the solid colors. Don't be afraid to use plain muslin to set off one or two blocks.

Try a textured print for visual appeal. Trees don't all have to be bright green, nor do their trunks have to be chocolate brown. Be sure to search through material in your fabric library or scrap bag. The important thing is to use colors and prints you really like in your special quilt.

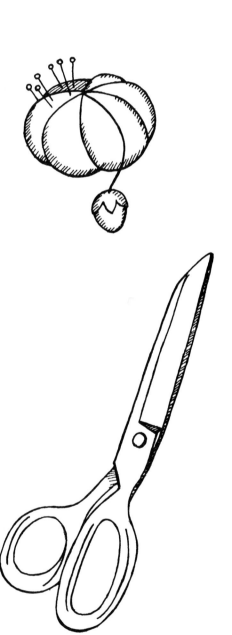

Fabric Requirements

Each of the twenty-two quilts in this book have yardages given for each piece if made just like the pattern. Be sure to adjust this if you choose to make your quilt larger or smaller. Almost all the quilts were made using a rotary cutter to cut strips on the crosswise grain and material requirements reflect this. Therefore, if a border strip is to be cut 68" long, there will be a seam in it, but it will not be easily seen in the finished quilt. If you wish seamless borders cut on the lengthwise grain, then buy more yardage than recommended. All quilts except the Bear Tree quilt have straight sewn borders. If you choose to miter the corners, additional yardage will be required. Add about 6" to each border piece. If you wish to have your quilt backing in one piece, you will need to purchase 85" or 90" muslin for backing. The samples in this book were made this way. It eliminates quilting over a seam and is easy to cut, leaving more time to quilt!

Feel free to change the size of any of these patterns. Perhaps you want a Fan Tree quilt for your bed. Determine the size you want, then use graph paper to compute the new size. Another way to change size is to widen the sashing strips, or make them narrower, or eliminate a row of blocks or borders.

Getting Ready

The importance of good preparation is a fact of life, whether climbing a mountain, cooking a delicious meal, or making a quilt. Certain tools are necessary to have an enjoyable and problem-free experience with your project. Some of the following items are a necessity, others are nice to have, but all are needed in some form.

Scissors

You will need two pairs of scissors: one pair for making accurate templates and for cutting paper and another for cutting fabric. Having only one pair is like mixing oil and water. Invest in a pair of good fabric-cutting scissors, remembering that long-term benefits always pay off. Eight to ten layers of fabric can easily be cut at one time without shifting. If necessary, put a padlock on the handles of your good scissors so the rest of the family will leave them alone, or hide them in a secret place.

Rotary Cutter and Mat

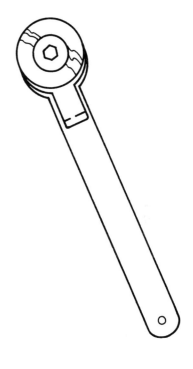

Many quilts at my house have been made without this time-saving device, but many more could have been made due to its accuracy and speed. Now, I cut almost everything with this aid. My quilts are more accurate and speedily made. There are a few templates to make, and almost no marking. Many mats are available now with a 1" grid which further cuts down on measuring.

Ruler

A transparent ruler is invaluable to the quilter. It is marked in 1/8" segments and lines can be drawn smoothly and accurately. An 18" is a must, and a 24" one is great for a straight edge with the rotary cutter. Getting a ruler the same brand as the rotary mat makes for even greater accuracy.

Pins

A box of quilter's pins is a big help. They are 1 3/4" long, strong, and used for pinning multiple layers of fabric, and aid in basting a quilt. I use them for all my other sewing as well. One nice thing to do for yourself is to throw away your short dull pins and get new ones.

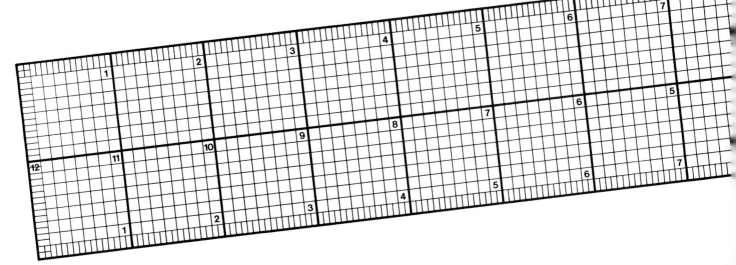

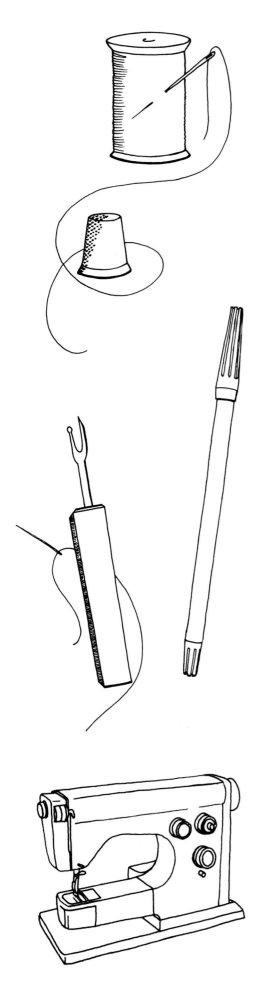

Needles

For basting a quilt, long soft sculpture needles are great. For applique, "betweens" are recommended, or embroidery needles that are easy to work with and have larger eyes to thread. For quilting, most quilters like a short #8 or #9 quilting needle. Embroidery needles also work well.

Thimble

Find a well-fitting thimble. Now is the time to learn to use one. A thimble prevents holes in fingertips and helps maintain sanity.

Markers

The invention of the water erasable marker is a boon to quilters for marking quilt patterns. It works like a felt pen and comes in several colors, yet will disappear when sprayed or washed with cold water.

Masking Tape

Masking tape in several sizes is good for marking straight lines to quilt. One-fourth-inch wide tape is especially invaluable to make a straight line exactly 1/4" from the seam line. It is reusable, inexpensive, and gives a quality touch to any quilt. Wider widths mark an even grid; quilt along the edge then move it on.

Drafting supplies

Graph paper is a necessity for designing or making accurate templates or patterns. Eight squares to the inch is just right. Tracing paper is a must for accurately copying a design from a book. A supply of manila folders, large file cards, x-ray film, and old cereal boxes can provide sources for making templates. A 6" transparent ruler and 45° angle also help.

Ironing Board and Iron

A standard steam iron and board are fine for quilting. Consider making your own ironing board if you sew a lot. Determine how much room you have, then buy an unfinished door to fit the space. A thirty-six-inch by seventy-two-inch door is a nice size to use. Drill a number of small holes for ventilation then cover with an old mattress pad and muslin, stretching to make the top smooth, and tack it to the back. It really helps to have a large padded surface to iron 45" or 60" material in one sweep. It also makes a fine surface on which to pin pieces of a block when deciding which fabrics to use. This board could be stored in a closet when not in use.

Sewing Machine

A sewing machine in good repair is the cornerstone to quilting. It need not be the latest design. Keep the needles sharp and change them frequently. Know your machine and master how it works. Determine the guidelines for a one-fourth-inch seam on both sides of the needle and mark with masking tape if necessary.

Washington Splendour, 94" x 114", is a tessellated tree pattern depicting the evergreens of the Cascade Mountains. Lighter trees along the diagonal achieve the effect of sunlight filtering through the forest. Directions for this quilt are on page 18.

Autumn Splendour, 50" x 54", is an explosion of vibrant fall colors. See page 20 for directions.

Whimsy Tree, 48" x 61", is reminiscent of a leisurely stroll down a maple-lined street. Page 58 gives directions.

Welcome the holiday season with this Woodland Christmas wall hanging, 18" x 24", outside your door. See directions on page 36. The Christmas Star Tree, below, 36" x 36", and the mini-Christmas Log Tree, below right, 18" x 25", are both based on the Log Cabin block. Both make nice wall quilts or gifts for the Christmas season. See pages 60 and 22.

12

The Log Tree, 72'' x 89'', is made from the traditional Log Cabin block. Here we see short trees with stubby trunks in a light background forest, but this design would be equally lovely in spring or fall shades. Directions on page 22.

13

The Bear Tree, above, 54" x 54", originated from the Bear Paw pattern and grew into a tree. Bears are quilted in the center of each tree. Quilting is by Ellie Strain. Directions are on page 50. The Love Tree, right, 44" x 58", is designed as a child's crib or lap quilt. This whimsical design will bring a smile to those who use it. Trees have feelings, so of course they must have hearts. Quilted by Peg Storey and Carol Seeger. Follow the directions on page 52.

Any of these tree wall hangings are sure to brighten your home. Forest Primeval, left, 44" x 44", will enhance any contemporary settings with its diamond shape and strong graphic lines. Quilted by Clarice Jacques. See page 41 for directions. The Quickie Strippy Tree, below, 18" x 28", is quickly stitched together on the machine using strips of fabric. See page 49. The Fan Tree, below left, 24" x 57", is based on the traditional Grandmother's Fan block and embellished with lace and hand quilting. Directions on page 55.

A dramatic quilt deserves dramatic accessories, and so it is with Autumn Glory, 81'' x 102''. This applique quilt done in glorious fall colors is shown with a coordinating muslin dust ruffle and pillow shams on a twig bed. See page 28. The twig clothes tree and plant stand carry through the design theme. Twig furniture from Willow Creek Creations, P.O. Box 394, Duvall, WA 98019.

Getting a Good Start

You have the proper tools and materials, and it is time to start. You have chosen the pattern and fabric, now what?

The templates in this book are carefully marked as to name of pattern, part of total pattern, and number of pieces to cut from each fabric. First, make templates from the patterns in the book. Check them with your ruler for accuracy. Carefully trace over each one with tracing paper, cut out just inside the pencil line, and glue with glue stick to cardboard or plastic. I like to use file cards, but plastic will stay more accurate through cutting many pieces. Check often with your ruler for accuracy. This is one of the most important parts of quilt making.

You are now ready to cut your preshrunk ironed fabric. You may choose to cut fabric by using one of several methods. Each piece may be cut individually by tracing around the template directly onto the cloth with a fine pencil or you may cut in strips with a rotary cutter and cut several pieces at one time. Whichever method you use, you must take the time to be accurate. To be off by even 1/16" grows into 1" every 16" and that can cause problems if your quilt is 82" long!

When sewing pieces together, press each seam before adding another one that crosses it. Press toward the darker fabric, or away from where you will quilt. You should know before you start where you will quilt to make the quilting easier. Careful pressing at this point saves time later.

You are now ready to follow the directions for the quilt of your choice.

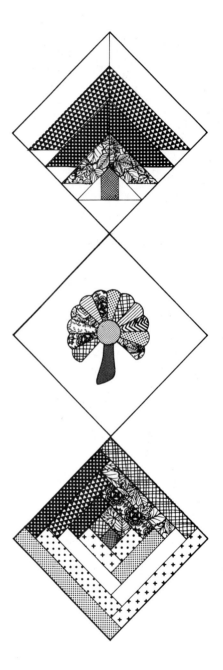

This section of the book contains directions and template patterns for twenty-two quilts in varying sizes. Templates are identified by quilt name, template number, and number of pieces to be cut from each fabric.

Several templates are labeled A and AR which means to cut a specified number like the template, then flip the template over and cut specified R or reversed pieces.

Fabric colors refer to the sample quilt. Refer to the color picture and then change colors if you wish.

All templates include a 1/4" seam allowance, as do the border cutting dimensions. Grain line is noted where needed. Several templates are printed with a fold line. Be sure to make these templates full size before cutting the fabric. In some cases, smaller pieces overlap larger pieces, so be sure to include the entire template, including the space covered by the smaller piece, when you make the larger templates.

Several patterns use letter or number designations and are cut from given dimensions, rather than providing templates. Therefore, not all patterns have templates for alphabet letters in sequence.

All borders are straight sewn except where a striped print is used; then corners are mitered.

Washington Splendour

This is the quilt that inspired me to think more about trees. The many shades of green in the Cascade Mountains have long challenged me to translate "real" trees into a quilt. Upon reading the book *Contemporary Quilts* by Kay Parker (©1981 The Crossing Press, Trumansburg, New York*), I discovered her tessellated tree pattern. Tessellation is defined as "a mosaic of a repeated design with no background."

In tracing the design from her book, I inadvertently set the second row to the right, half a block. Instead of trees on top of each other, they were now offset. The "upside-down" trees were a reflection of the previous row. What would happen if the trees were print fabric and the reflections were a matching solid? The result is Washington Splendour.

To achieve the effect of the sun filtering through the forest, I drew a diagonal line from the upper left corner to the lower right corner. The lightest trees are closest to this line and are progressively darker away from it to the corners. What fun it was to go to the fabric store and choose eleven shades of solid green plus thirty-five green and white prints!

To design your own special quilt, trace over the pattern on the title page of this book, then decide how to color your quilt. It will be easier than it sounds. Experiment with felt pens or colored pencils to achieve the effect you wish. Then start in! See color picture on page 9.

Forevergreen Pattern by Kay Parker with instructions and templates available for $3.25 from Kay Parker, P.O. Box 305, Ithaca, N.Y. 14851.

Size: 94" x 114"

Each tree is 8" x 12" with 11 trees across and 9 trees down.

Materials:

Scraps of green print and matching solids (1/4 yd. yields 4 trees, 1/2 yd. yields 8 trees, etc.)
7 1/2 yds. print for backing
Batting
1 yd. green solid for border
1 yd. white for binding

Directions:

1. Make Templates A-F.
2. From Quilt Piecing Guide you have traced from title page, determine the number of trees to cut from each color. Cut from prints and matching solids, using D-F reversed for half trees as needed.
3. From green solid for border, make 2 strips 3" x 108 1/2" and 2 strips 3" x 94 1/2". From backing fabric make a piece 96" x 116". From white for binding cut and sew 2 1/2" bias strips to make 435".
4. On floor or large table, arrange trees and reflections according to the Quilt Piecing Guide. Make any changes at this point.
5. Following Quilt Piecing Guide on title page, sew in horizontal rows. Sew 3 rows together for trees, carefully matching strips. Sew tree strips together for quilt top.
6. For border, sew a 108 1/2" strip to each side, then a 94 1/2" strip to top and bottom.
7. Cut and sew print for backing to make a piece 98" x 118".
8. Piece batting to make 98" x 118".
9. Position backing, batting, and top. Pin, baste, quilt, and bind according to quilting procedure in Glossary.

Quilting Suggestion: Quilt 1/4" around each print tree. Use leaf pattern in border.

Washington Splendour Templates

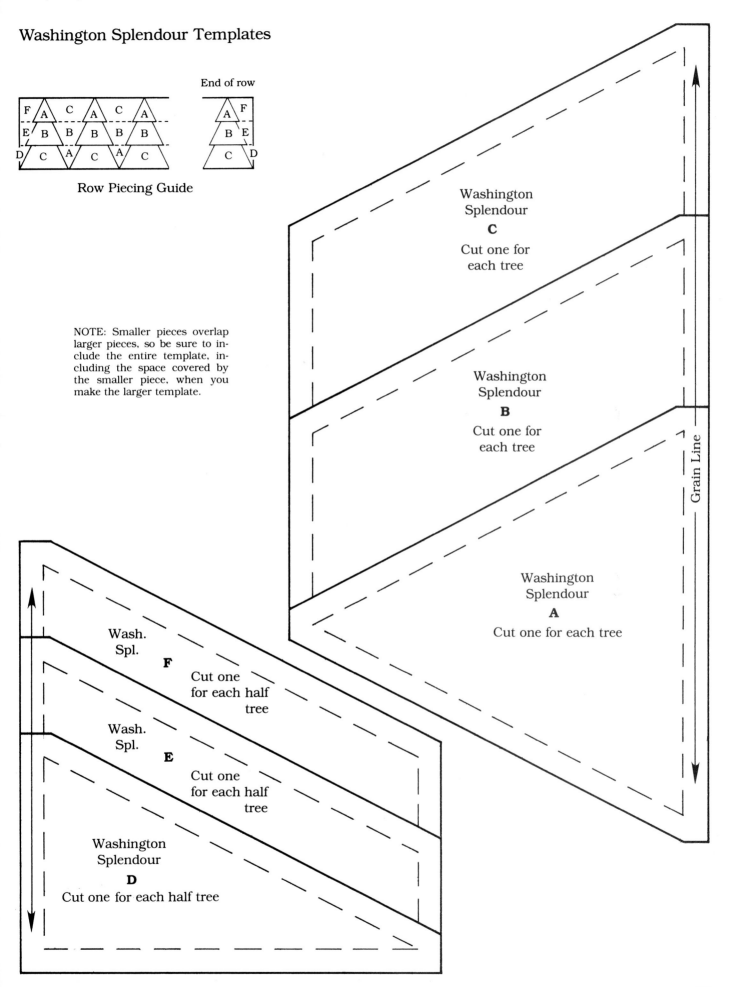

End of row

Row Piecing Guide

NOTE: Smaller pieces overlap larger pieces, so be sure to include the entire template, including the space covered by the smaller piece, when you make the larger template.

Washington
Splendour
C
Cut one for
each tree

Washington
Splendour
B
Cut one for
each tree

Washington
Splendour
A
Cut one for each tree

Grain Line

Wash.
Spl.
F
Cut one
for each half
tree

Wash.
Spl.
E
Cut one
for each half
tree

Washington
Splendour
D
Cut one for each half tree

Autumn Splendour

Autumn is a special time of year. The myriad colors in this season seems to be emphasized in trees. The vine maple of the Pacific Northwest exhibits every hue of the color spectrum, from fluorescent yellow to chocolate brown.

This quilt is an explosion of these vibrant colors. Trace your own Quilt Piecing Guide from the Title Page and experiment with colored pens or pencils until you have colors that reflect what you like.

The sample quilt starts with a glowing yellow in the center and ends with brown in the corners. It is quite striking. Page 10 shows this quilt in color.

Size: 50" x 54"

Materials:

Print and matching solid scraps to make 84 full trees and 8 half trees in the following colors:

10 yellow	5 dark red
9 gold	16 rust
10 orange	12 brown
22 red	8 brown half trees

1 yd. brown solid for first border and binding
2/3 yd. brown print for second border
2 1/3 yds. brown print for backing
Batting

Directions:

1. Make Templates A-F.
2. Cut 1 each of A, B, and C from print and matching solid:

10 yellow	5 dark red
9 gold	16 rust
10 orange	12 brown
22 red	

Cut 4 D, E, F, and 4 D, E, F reversed from brown prints and solids. Note: each print tree has its matching solid reflection. The reflections for the bottom trees are cut to match the prints for the bottom row, but will be sewn for the solid pieces in the top row.

From brown solid, for first border, make 2 strips 1 1/2" x 48 1/2" for sides and 2 strips 1 1/2" x 46 1/2" for top and bottom. Cut and sew 2 1/2" bias strips to make 220".

From brown print for second border make 4 strips 2 1/2" x 50 1/2".

From brown print for backing make backing 54" x 58".

From batting cut a piece 54" x 58".

3. Following Quilt Piecing Guide on page 21, arrange trees and reflections on large table or floor until you are satisfied with the result.

4. Sew 3 horizontal rows to make tree strip, then sew tree strips together for top.

5. For first border, sew a 48 1/2" strip to each side, then a 46 1/2" strip to top and bottom.

6. For second border, sew a 50 1/2" strip to each side, then a 50 1/2" strip to top and bottom.

7. Position backing, batting, and top. Pin, baste, quilt, and bind according to quilting procedure in Glossary.

Quilting Suggestion: Quilt around each tree as close as possible.

The righteous shall be like trees planted by the rivers of water and shall bring forth fruit in its season. -- King David

20

Autumn Splendour Templates

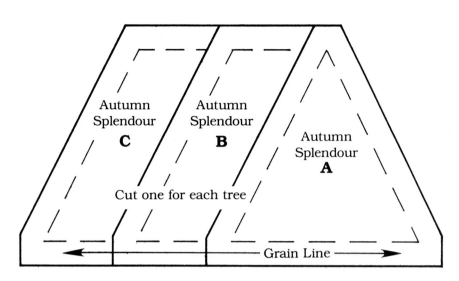

Autumn Splendour **C**

Autumn Splendour **B**

Autumn Splendour **A**

Cut one for each tree

Grain Line

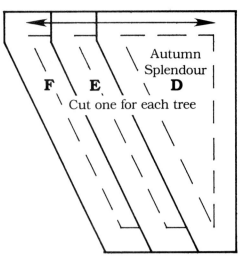

F **E** Autumn Splendour **D**

Cut one for each tree

NOTE: Smaller pieces overlap larger pieces, so be sure to include the entire template, including the space covered by the smaller piece, when you make the larger template.

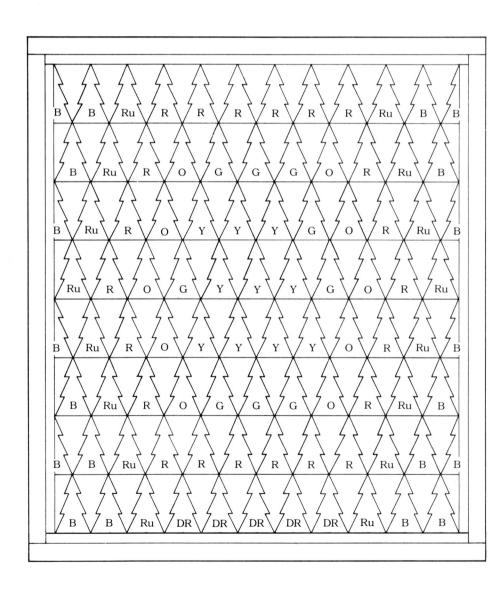

Autumn Splendour Quilt Piecing Guide and Suggested Color Placement 50 x 54

Y = Yellow
G = Gold
O = Orange
R = Red
DR = Dark red
Ru = Rust
B = Brown

The Log Tree

The Log Cabin is one of the most popular and versatile of the traditional patterns. The blocks of half light and half dark fabrics can be arranged in many configurations, depending on what pleases you the most.

How can this well-known, simply constructed but complex design be a tree?

The sample shows a squatty tree with a stubby trunk in a light background forest. It is done in dark greens, but would be equally as beautiful in shades of sage, spring green, or vibrant fall colors. Enjoy white snow-covered trees by turning the quilt upside down (the green can be the tree's shadow), or use Christmas prints for a forest of Christmas trees. In any case, make and enjoy your own special forest. See in color on page 13.

Size: 72" x 89"

There are 24 blocks to make using 4 light and 4 dark prints. Each block uses 2 pieces from each print.

Materials:

1/3 yd. dark print A	1/2 yd. light print A
1/2 yd. dark print B	2/3 yd. light print B
1/2 yd. dark print C	2/3 yd. light print C
2/3 yd. dark print D	7/8 yd. light print D

1/4 yd. red print for trunks
1/4 yd. muslin for first border
1 1/2 yds. green solid for second border
3/4 yd. white for bias
Batting
4 1/2 yds. green print for backing

Directions:

No templates are used in this pattern: this is an exception in this book. 1/4" seam allowance is included in all measurements.

From red print for trunks cut 24, 2" squares.

From dark and light prints, cut 24, 2" strips into the following lengths:

Dark print A: #1 - 2"
           #6 - 6 1/2"
Dark print B: #2 - 3 1/2"
           #13 - 11"
Dark print C: #5 - 5"
           #10 - 9 1/2"
Dark print D: #9 - 8"
           #14 - 12 1/2"
Light print A: #3 - 3 1/2"
           #8 - 8"
Light print B: #4 - 5"
           #15 - 12 1/2"
Light print C: #7 - 6 1/2"
           #12 - 11"
Light print D: #11 - 9 1/2"
           #16 - 14"

From muslin for first border, make 2 strips 3/4" x 76" and 2 strips 3/4" x 58".

From green solid for second border, make 2 strips 6 1/2" x 77" and 2 strips 6 1/2" x 71".

From white for bias, cut and sew 2 1/2" bias strips to make 325".

From green print for backing, make a piece 76" x 94".

1. Using the Block Piecing Guide for placement and starting with red trunk piece and #1 dark print, sew the 16 numbered pieces in sequence, working clockwise, taking 1/4" seams and pressing after each seam. Make 24 blocks.

2. To make fill-in blocks for edges of quilt, place blocks on point as in diagram and carefully cut (a) 3 blocks vertically down center, (b) 2 blocks horizontally, (c) 1 block both vertically and horizontally.

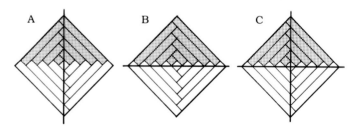

3. Sew blocks and fill-in blocks according to photograph, carefully matching edge blocks to keep pattern sequence.

4. For first border, sew a 76" muslin strip to each side, then a 58" strip to top and bottom.

5. For second border, sew a 77" green strip to each side, then a 71" strip to top and bottom.

6. Position backing, batting, and top. Pin, baste, quilt, and bind according to quilting procedure in glossary.

Quilting Suggestion: Quilt through the center of each log and around red square in each block. Three-fourths-inch masking tape makes a good guide.

Note: When working with narrow borders and seams, concentrate on strip width instead of seam allowance on right.

This log cabin is designed for quick, uncomplicated assembly using one method of piecing for all blocks. By making all blocks the same and cutting the fill-in blocks, the seam allowance is cut off, but is made up for since the cut is on the bias. This simplifies construction all the way through.

In the picture on page 12 there is a mini-Christmas Log Tree. Follow the above directions, except cut 1" square for center and fabric for logs 1" wide, varying in length. The finished logs will be 1/2" wide and the overall size will be 18" x 25". This makes a nice small wall quilt for the Christmas season. You may wish to use Christmas prints.

The Log Tree
Block Piecing Guide

Top

				DkB 13				
LtD 16	LtC 12	LtA 8	LtB 4	DkD 9				
				DkC 5				
				DkA 1 / Red	DkB 2	DkA 6	DkC 10	DkD 14
				LtA 3				
				LtC 7				
				LtD 11				
				LtB 15				

Color Placement

Forest Simplicica

Thirteen pieced print blocks alternate with twelve solid blocks to make this unique quilt. Each solid block features four quilted trees. The bright sashing separates the trees in this forest, making the pieced trees stand in a grandeur all their own. The quilting pattern can also be used with the trunks meeting in the center. These evergreens will add life to any setting. Page 88 shows this quilt in color.

Size: 78" x 78"

Materials:

2 1/2 yds. muslin for solid blocks, background, and first border
1 1/4" yd. bright green print for corners and second border
5/8 yd. medium green print for tree tops
1/2 yd. dark green print for tree bottoms
1/8 yd. brown print for trunks
2 1/2 yds. solid green for sashing and bias binding
Batting
4 2/3 yds. print for backing

Directions:

1. Make Templates A-E, extending C and D on fold line.
2. Cut as directed on templates. In addition:
   From bright print for second border make 2 strips 3 1/2" x 73" for sides, and 2 strips 3 1/2" x 79" for top and bottom.
   From muslin for solid blocks, cut 12, 12 1/2" squares. For first border make 2 strips 3/4" x 72 1/2" for sides and 2 strips 3/4" x 73" for top and bottom.
   From solid green for sashing, cut 20 strips 2 1/2" x 12 1/2".
   Make 6 strips 2 1/2" x 68 1/2" for sides and 2 strips 2 1/2" x 72 1/2" for top and bottom.
   Cut and sew 2 1/2" bias strips to make 315".
   From print for backing, make an 82" square.
   From batting, cut an 82" square.
3. Using Block Piecing Guide, sew 13 blocks.
4. On floor or table, arrange pieced and solid blocks according to photograph. Add 20, 12 1/2" and 4, 68 1/2" sashing strips and sew together in rows. Join rows for top.
5. Sew a 2 1/2" x 68 1/2" strip to each side, then a 2 1/2" x 72 1/2" strip to top and bottom.
6. From white for first border sew a 3/4" x 72 1/2" strip to each side, then a 3/4" x 73" strip to top and bottom. Concentrate on strip width on left instead of seam allowance on right to obtain an even 1/4" wide border.
7. From bright green for second border, sew a 3 1/2" x 79" strip to each side, then a 3 1/2" x 73" strip to top and bottom.
8. Position backing, batting, and top. Pin, baste, quilt, and bind according to quilting procedure in Glossary.

Quilting Suggestion: Quilt 4 tree patterns, given on page 61, in each plain block, with either trunks or tree tops at center. Outline quilt each piece on pieced blocks.

Block Piecing Guide

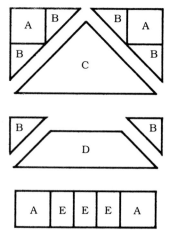

The trees of the wood sing out for joy
-- King David

24

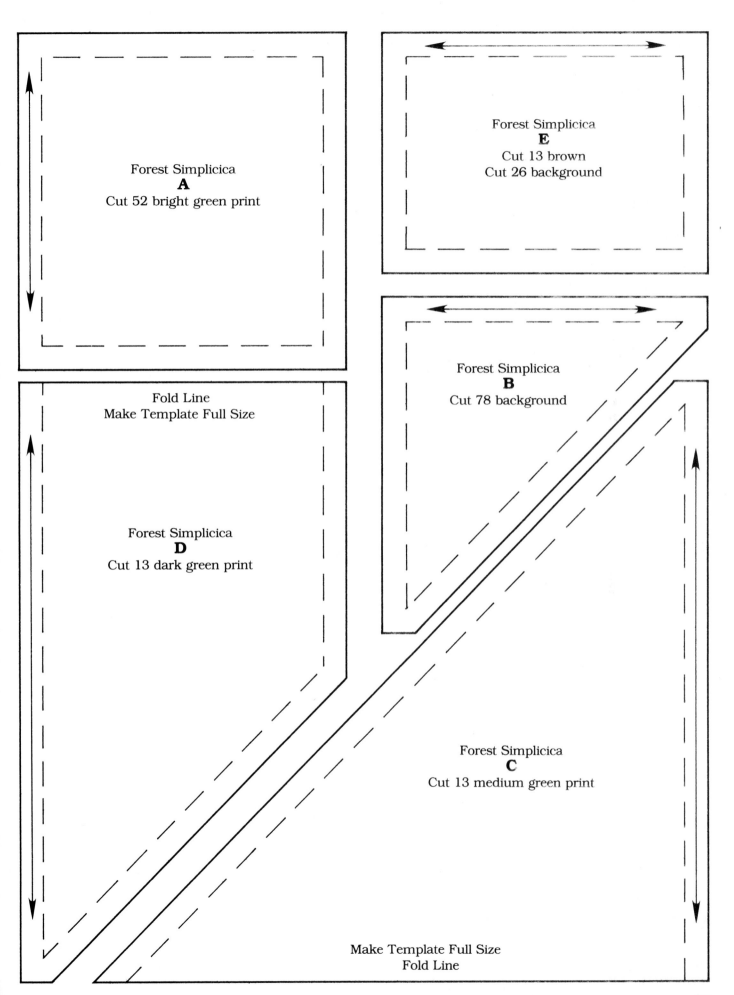

Forest Simplicica
A
Cut 52 bright green print

Forest Simplicica
E
Cut 13 brown
Cut 26 background

Fold Line
Make Template Full Size

Forest Simplicica
B
Cut 78 background

Forest Simplicica
D
Cut 13 dark green print

Forest Simplicica
C
Cut 13 medium green print

Make Template Full Size
Fold Line

The Simply Tree

This quilt with large blocks is designed for the beginner. It can also be used by the intermediate or advanced quilter who would like to strip piece or make the tree shape from tiny triangles using a variety of prints or scraps. The tree shape is basic so any composite of shapes or colors may be used. An autumn tree quilt using oranges, rusts, and browns would add warmth to any room. Choose muted blues or grays for a cool look, or bright green and yellow to add snap to a cool corner. Another way to use color effectively would be to make the center tree the lightest shade, working out to the darkest shades in the corners. The quilt would also be striking with an all off-white muslin background, making the trees appear to "float." For variety, turn the quilt upside down to enjoy solid color trees. Experiment with colors to obtain the effect you wish. The sample quilt is made using five shades of green prints and solids with the top row the lightest shade and the darkest shade at the bottom. See page 86.

Size: 68" x 82"

Materials:

1/4 yd. brown print for trunks
3/8 yd. each of 5 prints for trees
5/8 yd. each of 5 matching solids for background
1/4 yd. white for first border
1 1/4 yds. brown solid for second border and binding
5/8 yd. medium green for third border
4 1/2 yds. print for backing
Batting

Directions:

1. Make Templates A and B as follows. Add 1/4" seam allowance.

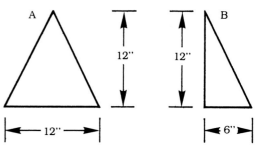

Make Templates C-F.

2. Note that row 1 is the top horizontal row.

From each of 5 prints for rows, 1, 3, and 5 cut 5 A; Rows 2 and 4 cut 4 A, 1 B, 1 B reversed.

From each of 5 matching solids for rows 1, 3, and 5 cut 4 A, 1 B, 1 B reversed, 4 C, 2 D. Rows 2 and 4 cut 5 A, 5 C

From brown print for trunks cut 23 E, 4 F.

From white for first border make 2 strips 3/4" x 75 1/2" for sides and 2 strips 3/4" x 61" for top and bottom.

From brown solid for second border make 2 strips 1 1/2" x 76" for sides and 2 strips 1 1/2" x 63" for top and bottom.

From medium green solid for third border, make 2 strips 2 1/2" x 78" for sides and 2 strips 2 1/2" x 67" for top and bottom.

From remaining brown solid for binding, cut and sew 2 1/2" bias strips to make 315".

3. Starting with top tree row (row 1) and following photograph, sew 5 prints A alternately with 4 matching solids A, starting and ending with 1 solid B.

4. Sew tree rows 2 and 4, using 4 prints A alternately with 5 matching solids A, starting and ending with 1 print B.

5. For trunk rows 1, 3, and 5, sew 5 E alternately with 4 matching solids C, starting and ending with D.

6. For trunk rows 2 and 4, sew 5 matching solids C alternately with 4 E starting and ending with F.

7. Sew 5 trunk strips to matching tree strips.

8. Sew completed tree strips in rows taking care to match points on sides and tops of trees.

9. For first border, sew a 75 1/2" white strip to each side, then sew a 61" strip to top and bottom.

10. For second border, sew a 76" brown strip to each side, then sew a 63" strip to top and bottom.

11. For third border, sew a 78" green strip to each side then a 67" strip to top and bottom.

12. Seam backing as needed to make a piece 74" x 86".

13. Position backing, batting, and top. Pin, baste, quilt, and bind according to quilting procedure in Glossary.

Quilting Suggestion: Quilt 2" wide V's in each print and solid tree. You might wish to extend lines down into trunk row.

Dresden Tree Templates

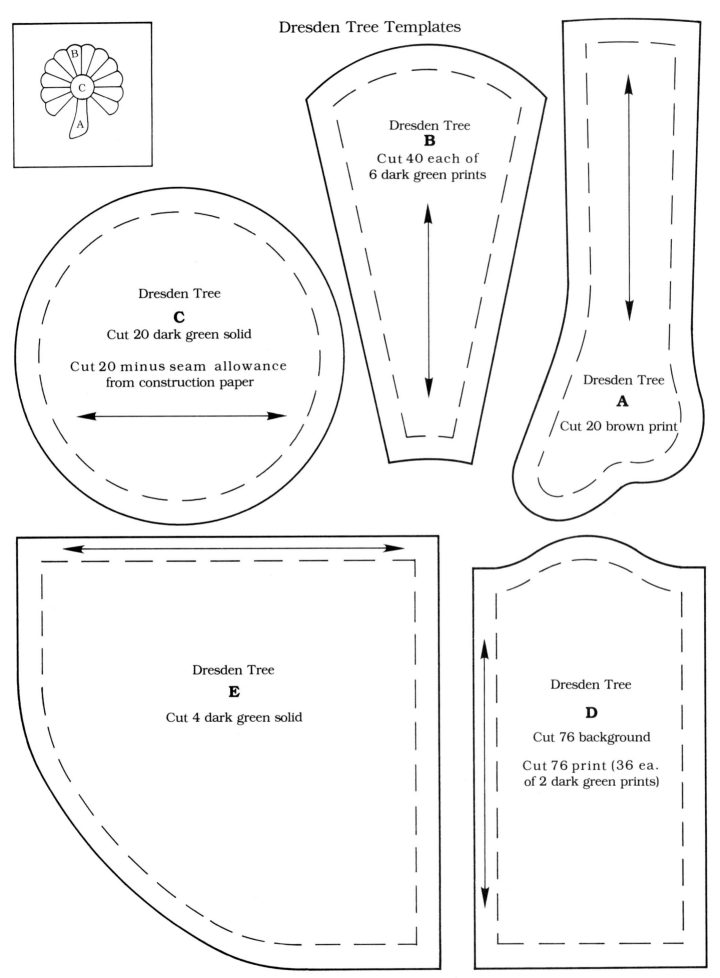

Dresden Tree
B
Cut 40 each of
6 dark green prints

Dresden Tree
C
Cut 20 dark green solid

Cut 20 minus seam allowance
from construction paper

Dresden Tree
A
Cut 20 brown print

Dresden Tree
E
Cut 4 dark green solid

Dresden Tree
D
Cut 76 background

Cut 76 print (36 ea.
of 2 dark green prints)

The Raintree

In the Pacific Northwest is an area known as the rain forest. Here the sun does not penetrate the dense forest and rainfall is ample, producing a tropical atmosphere. Moss grows profusely, hanging from trees like icicles in winter. These long flowing strands of moss make the trees look like weeping willows. The Raintree design reminds me of these trees. The appliqued vines and leaves also add character. The ribbon border is a favorite of mine and suggests many trees guarding this special forest. This quilt provides a variety of techniques for the quilter -- the log cabin-like raintrees in the center, intricate quilting designs in the alternate blocks, a sawtooth pieced border around the medallion, appliqued leaves and vines, and the challenge of multipieced trees in the ribbon border.

This quilt has it all and provides an opportunity to try a number of techniques. Although not a quilt-in-a-day project, creating this quilt will grow on you, just like the rain forest for which it is named! See page 83 for picture in color.

Size: 78" x 78"

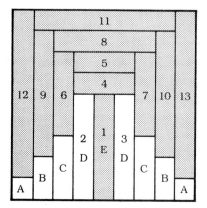

Block Piecing Guide

Materials:

2/3 yd. muslin for tree blocks and sawtooth border

1/8 yd. brown print for tree block trunks

1 yd. darkest green print for tree blocks, vine, and ribbon borders

1/4 yd. next darkest green print for tree blocks

1/4 yd. medium green print for tree blocks

1 yd. light green print for tree blocks and ribbon border

3 1/3 yds. dark green solid for tree blocks, solid borders, sawtooth border, vine and ribbon borders, and bias binding

3 2/3 yds. green-on-white background for alternate blocks, vine border, and ribbon border

4 2/3 yds. green print for backing

Batting

Construction paper for paper piecing

Note: To simplify cutting and assembly, this quilt is divided into 6 sections and will be referred to by section name. The sections are:

1. Tree blocks -- Nine 9" pieced trees with green solid borders.

2. Alternate blocks -- Four green-on-white background blocks, 8 half blocks, and 4 corner blocks that alternate with the tree blocks to make a medallion.

3. Green solid borders -- Five green solid borders named first solid border, second solid border, etc.

4. Sawtooth border -- Ninety-six muslin and green solid sawtooth segments which frame the medallion.

5. Vine borders -- Dark green solid vines and dark green print leaves appliqued on green-on-white background print. These are known as first vine border, second vine border, third vine border, and form the corners.

6. Ribbon border -- Outer quilt border made of Units A and B with corner blocks.

Quilt Piecing Guide (detail of 1/4 of quilt)

Directions:

1. Make templates for alternate blocks F and G. Add 1/4" seam allowance on all sides.

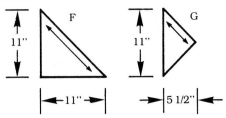

2. Use Vine Border Diagram on page 35 to make a full-size Placement Guide from paper. Cut paper into Vine Border segments and add 1/4" seam allowance to make templates. Cut 4 of each Vine Border Segment from green and white background fabric.

3. Make Templates H, J, K, L, LR, M, N

4. Cut fabric as follows:

From muslin for tree blocks cut

18 A -- 1 1/2" x 1 1/2"	18 C -- 1 1/2" x 3 1/2"
18 B -- 1 1/2" x 2 1/2"	18 D -- 1 1/2" x 5 1/2"

Note: To simplify directions, several templates use letter or number designations and are cut from given dimensions, rather than providing templates.

From muslin for sawtooth cut 96 H

From brown print for tree blocks cut 9 E -- 1 1/2" x 5 1/2"

From darkest green print for tree blocks cut
    9 #4 -- 1 1/2" x 3 1/2"
    for vine cut 88 J
    for ribbon cut 70 L reversed

From next darkest green print for tree blocks cut
    9 #5 -- 1 1/2" x 3 1/2"
    18 #6 and #7 -- 1 1/2" x 4 1/2"

From medium green print for tree blocks cut
    9 #8 -- 1 1/2" x 5 1/2"
    18 #9 and #10 -- 1 1/2" x 6 1/2"

From light green print for tree blocks cut
    9 #11 -- 1 1/2" x 7 1/2"
    18 #12 and #13 -- 1 1/2" x 8 1/2"
    for ribbon border cut 70 L

From dark green solid for tree block borders cut
    18 -- 1 1/2" x 9 1/2" for sides
    18 -- 1 1/2" x 11 1/2" for top and bottom

For solid borders cut and sew to make strips for:
    First border -- 2 strips 1 1/2" x 46 1/2" for sides
    --2 strips 1 1/2" x 48 1/2" for top and bottom
    Second border -- 4 strips 1 1/2" x 50"
    Third border -- 4 strips 1 1/2" x 30"
    Fourth border -- 4 strips 1 1/2" x 18"
    Fifth border -- 2 strips 1 1/2" x 68 1/2" for sides -- 2
        strips 1 1/2" x 70 1/2" for top and bottom
    Sawtooth border 96 H
    Ribbon border 280 M, 4 N
    2 1/2" bias strips for binding to measure 325"
    3/4" bias strips to measure 256"

From green-on-white background fabric, for alternate blocks cut 4, 11 1/2" blocks, 8 F, and 4 G

Vine border background -- using paper pattern from step 2 above, cut 4 pieces of vine border background #1, #2, and #3

    For ribbon border cut 280 M, 4 N

From construction paper cut 88 K

5. Following Block Piecing Guide, sew 9 tree blocks by sewing pieces A, B, and C to appropriate strips, then sew in numerical sequence.

6. Sew a 9 1/2" green solid tree block border strip to each side, then an 11 1/2" strip to top and bottom of each block.

7. Following photograph, sew tree blocks to alternate blocks F and G.

8. Add first green solid border by sewing a 46 1/2" strip to opposite sides, then a 48 1/2" strip to remaining sides.

9. Following Quilt Piecing Guide for sawtooth border, make 4 rows of 24 squares each by joining muslin and dark green solid H. Join to first solid border. Remove last muslin H on rows at top and bottom.

10. Add second green solid border by sewing a 50" strip to each side, then a 50" strip to top and bottom. Trim sides according to diagram on page 35.

11. Make bias strip from 3/4" bias as follows. Fold and press 1/4" along each edge. Baste. Applique in curvy line on the 12 vine background border pieces.

12. Baste dark green print leaves J to construction paper K, following Paper Patch Applique instructions in Glossary.

13. Following Quilt Piecing Guide, applique paper pieced leaves on vine border pieces in a pleasing arrangement.

14. Following the Vine Border Diagram, sew first vine border to third solid border; add second vine border, fourth solid border, and third vine border. Now sew each complete vine border unit to second solid border.

15. For fifth green solid border, sew a 68 1/2" strip to each side, then a 70 1/2" strip to top and bottom.

16. Sew 70 Units A, then 70 Units B.

17. Sew 18 Units A alternately with 17 Units B, beginning and ending with Unit A. Make 4 of these strips.

18. Sew 1 of these ribbon strips to each side of quilt.

19. For corners, sew 1 dark green solid N to 1 green-on-white N. Following Quilt Piecing Guide, sew 1 of these blocks to each end of remaining 2 ribbon border strips, then sew strips to quilt top and bottom.

20. Cut and sew print backing to make a piece 82" square.

21. Position backing, batting and top. Pin, baste, quilt and bind according to quilting procedure in Glossary.

Quilting Suggestion: Choose intricate designs for alternate squares. Quilt with dark green thread and design will stand out even more. Quilt around each log on tree blocks, each sawtooth, border, vine, and leaves. For ribbon border, quilt a 2-line zigzag on either side of L and L reversed.

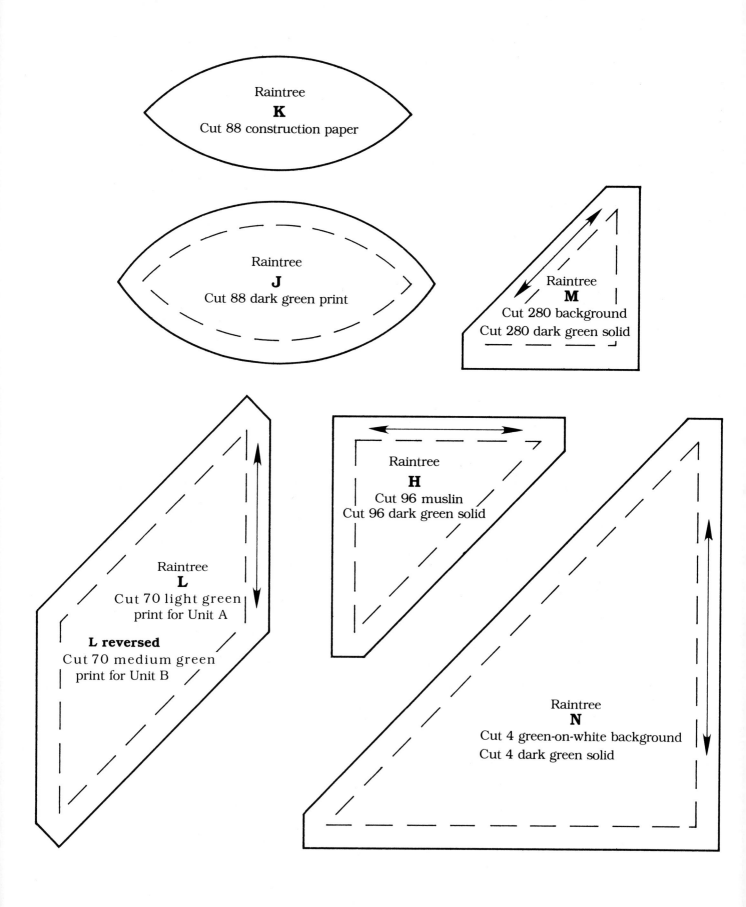

Raintree
K
Cut 88 construction paper

Raintree
J
Cut 88 dark green print

Raintree
M
Cut 280 background
Cut 280 dark green solid

Raintree
L
Cut 70 light green
print for Unit A

L reversed
Cut 70 medium green
print for Unit B

Raintree
H
Cut 96 muslin
Cut 96 dark green solid

Raintree
N
Cut 4 green-on-white background
Cut 4 dark green solid

The Raintree
Ribbon Border Template Placement

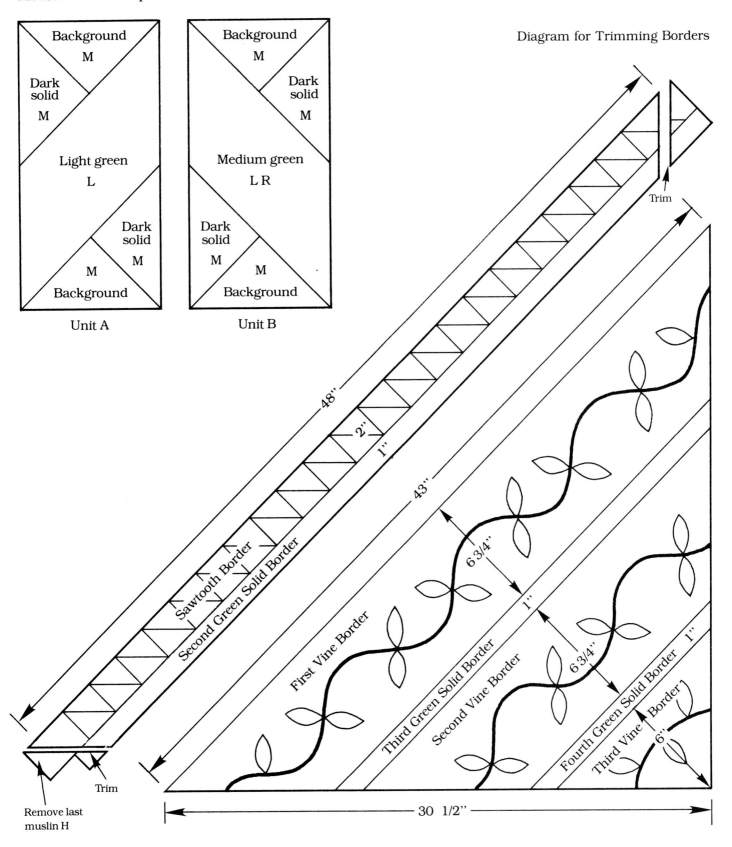

Diagram for Trimming Borders

Unit A

Unit B

Vine Border Diagram
Add seam allowance to each piece

The Woodland Tree

Squatty evergreens among the traditional "Puss-in-the-Corner" blocks make this design suitable for a crib or wall quilt as well as for a full-size bed. Different size templates are included for each.

This quilt also lends itself to using a variety of greens for the trees, making it a scrap quilt. Of course, no one says the trees have to be green. Note the Woodland Christmas wall hanging on page 12. It is made of seven tree blocks and eight Puss-in-the-Corner blocks and measures 18" x 24". Color picture on page 84.

Size: Wall quilt (4" blocks) 38" x 56"
Full-size Quilt (8" blocks) 76" x 112"

Materials:
Materials are for a wall quilt; those for a full-size bed quilt are in parentheses.
1/4 yd. (3/4 yd.) dark green print for trees
1/8 yd. (1/4 yd.) brown print for trunks
1 yd. (2 1/2 yds.) muslin for background
1/4 yd. (1/2 yd.) bright green print for center of block 2
1 1/3 yd. (2 1/2 yds.) light green solid for first border, corners of block 2, and binding
1/2 yd. (1 1/2 yd.) dark green print for second border
1 2/3 yd. (6 1/2 yds.) print for backing
Batting

Directions:
Directions are for a wall quilt; those for a full-size bed quilt are in parentheses.
1. Make Templates A-D for block 1 and A-C for block 2.
2. Cut as directed on template. In addition:
From light green solid for first border make 2 strips 2 1/2" x 36 1/2" (4 1/2" x 72 1/2") for sides and 2 strips 2 1/2" x 32 1/2" (4 1/2" x 64 1/2") for top and bottom. Cut and sew 2 1/2" bias strips to make 200" (386").
From dark green print for second border make 2 strips 3 1/2" x 40 1/2" (6 1/2" x 80 1/2") for sides and 2 strips 3 1/2" x 38 1/2" (6 1/2" x 76 1/2") for top and bottom.
From print for backing, make backing 42" x 60" (80" x 116").
3. Using Block Piecing Guide, sew 31 blocks 1 and 32 blocks 2.
4. Arrange blocks according to photograph and sew together, alternating blocks 1 and 2.
5. For first border, sew a 36 1/2" (72 1/2") strip to each side, then a 32 1/2" (64 1/2") strip to top and bottom.
6. For second border, sew a 40 1/2" (80 1/2") strip to each side, then a 38 1/2" (76 1/2") strip to top and bottom.
7. Position backing, batting and top. Pin, baste, quilt, and bind according to quilting procedure in Glossary.

Quilting Suggestion: Quilt around each tree and diagonally through each puss-in-the-corner block to bring out the tree design. The alternate blocks will frame each tree diagonally.

Woodland #1
(4" block)

Woodland-Alpine #2
(4" block)

Woodland #1
(8" block)

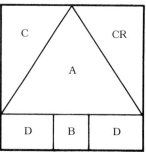

Woodland-Alpine #2
(8" block)

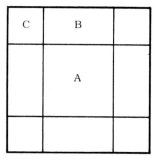

Let all the trees of the wood shout for joy
-- King David

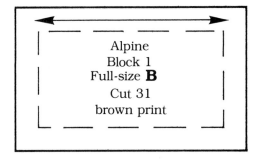

Alpine
Block 1
Full-size **B**
Cut 31
brown print

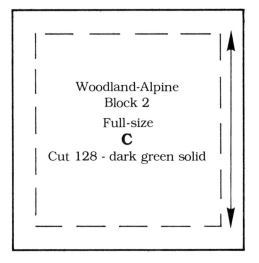

Woodland-Alpine
Block 2

Full-size
C
Cut 128 - dark green solid

The Alpine Tree

This tree is named after the alpine trees that live high in the mountains above the snow line. They have a very short growing season because of so much snow, therefore they are skinnier than those evergreens that live at lower elevations.

This design, like the Woodland Tree, has alpine blocks that alternate with Puss-in-the-Corner blocks. The use of Christmas prints for the trees makes them appear to be already decorated for the season. Experiment with prints and colors to achieve the effect you like best.

The materials and directions are the same as the Woodland Tree, and this quilt can also be made as a wall quilt or full-size quilt. Color picture on page 84.

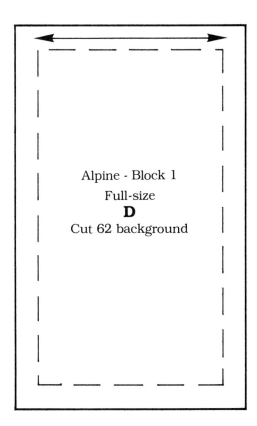

Alpine - Block 1
Full-size
D
Cut 62 background

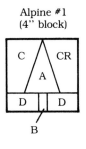

Alpine #1
(4" block)

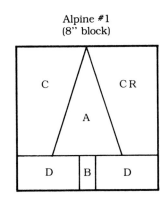

Alpine #1
(8" block)

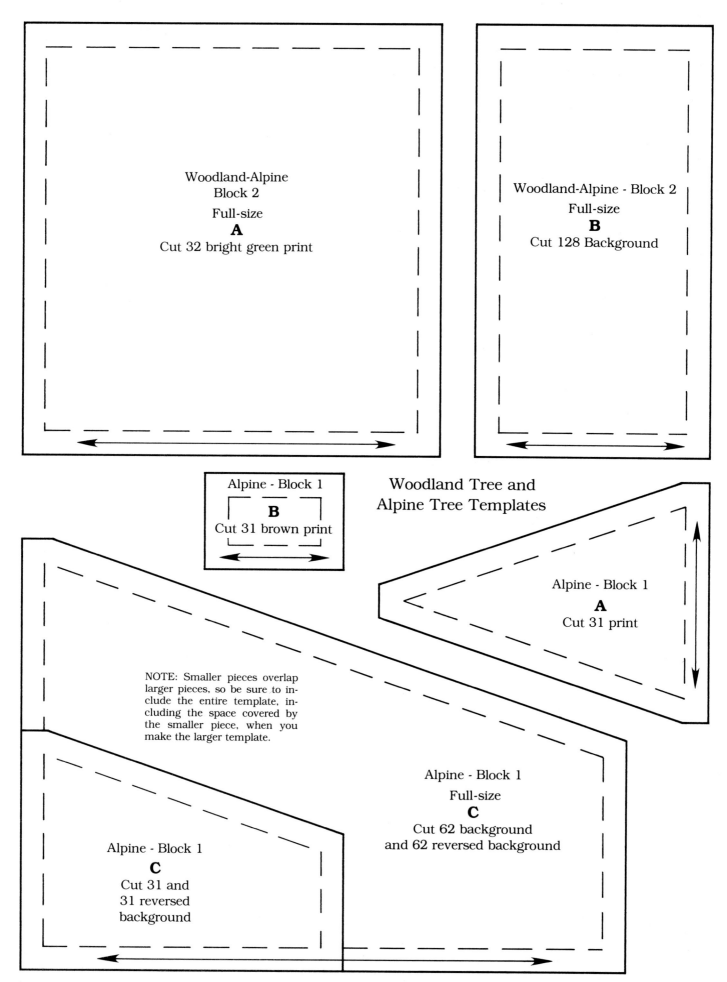

Woodland-Alpine
Block 2
Full-size
A
Cut 32 bright green print

Woodland-Alpine - Block 2
Full-size
B
Cut 128 Background

Alpine - Block 1
B
Cut 31 brown print

Woodland Tree and
Alpine Tree Templates

Alpine - Block 1
A
Cut 31 print

NOTE: Smaller pieces overlap
larger pieces, so be sure to include the entire template, including the space covered by
the smaller piece, when you
make the larger template.

Alpine - Block 1
Full-size
C
Cut 62 background
and 62 reversed background

Alpine - Block 1
C
Cut 31 and
31 reversed
background

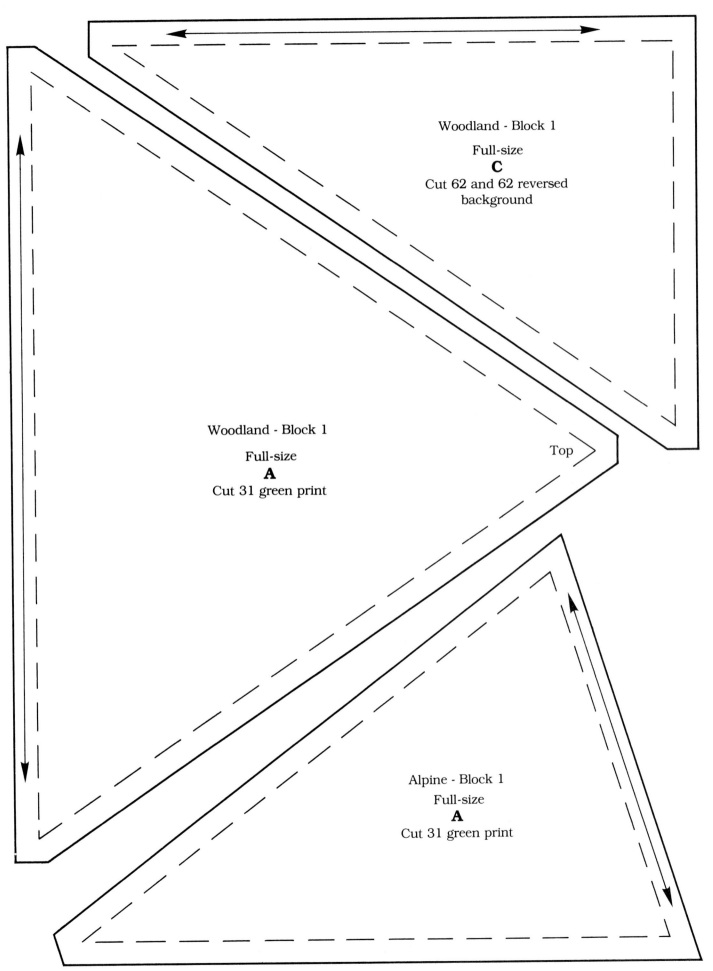

Woodland - Block 1

Full-size
C
Cut 62 and 62 reversed
background

Woodland - Block 1

Full-size
A
Cut 31 green print

Top

Alpine - Block 1

Full-size
A
Cut 31 green print

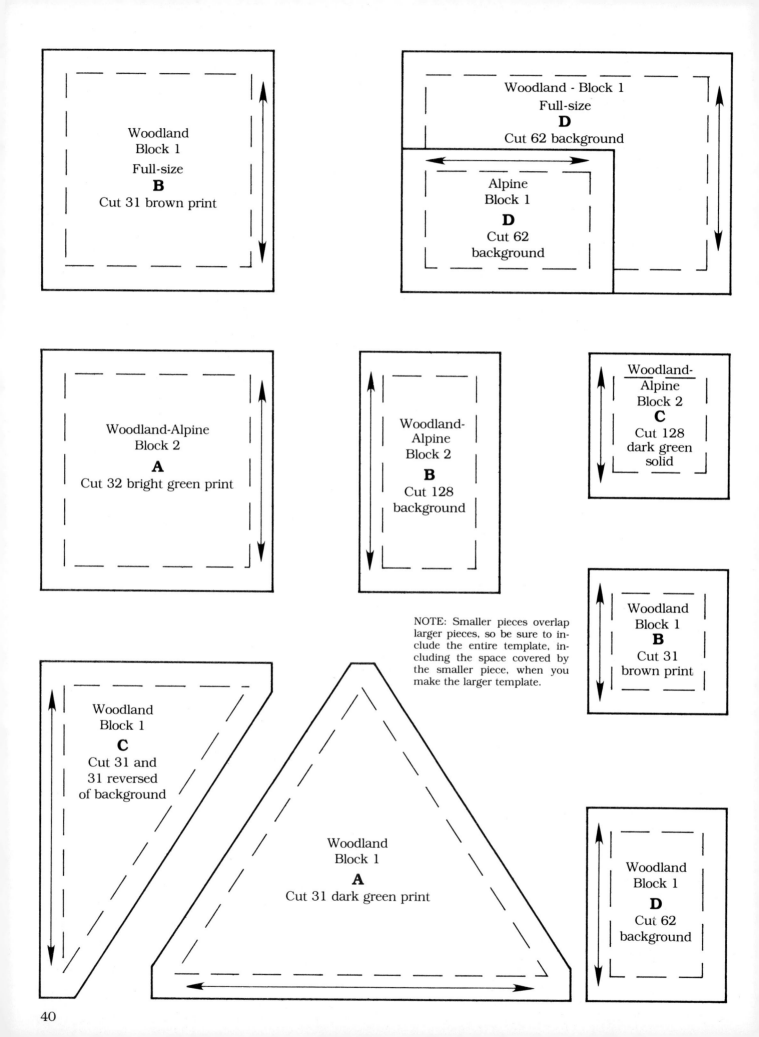

Woodland
Block 1

Full-size

B

Cut 31 brown print

Woodland - Block 1
Full-size
D
Cut 62 background

Alpine
Block 1

D

Cut 62
background

Woodland-Alpine
Block 2

A

Cut 32 bright green print

Woodland-
Alpine
Block 2

B

Cut 128
background

Woodland-
Alpine
Block 2

C

Cut 128
dark green
solid

Woodland
Block 1

B

Cut 31
brown print

NOTE: Smaller pieces overlap larger pieces, so be sure to include the entire template, including the space covered by the smaller piece, when you make the larger template.

Woodland
Block 1

C

Cut 31 and
31 reversed
of background

Woodland
Block 1

A

Cut 31 dark green print

Woodland
Block 1

D

Cut 62
background

Forest Primeval

This design provides countless adventures for the eye, whether hung on a wall or used as a small quilt. Start by looking at the bottom corner and you will discover there are many ways to get to the top. This tree is a variation of the old sawtooth tree. This quilt is easy and fun to put together. See page 15 for color photo.

Size: 44" x 44"

Materials:

3/4 yd. darkest green print for lower branch and second border
1/4 yd. next darkest print for middle branch
1/4 yd. lightest dark print for top branch
1 3/4 yd. muslin for background
1/4 yd. brown for trunk
2 yds. dark green solid for block borders, pieced sashing, first border and binding
1 1/2 yds. green print for backing
Batting

Break forth into singing, you mountains, O forest, and every tree in it. -- Isaiah

Directions:

1. Make Templates A-N.
2. Cut as directed on templates. In addition:
   From dark green solid for block borders cut 8 pieces 1 1/2" x 12 1/2" and 8 pieces 1 1/2" x 14 1/2". For first border, cut 2 pieces 1 1/2" x 37 1/2" for sides and 2 pieces 1 1/2" x 39 1/2" for top and bottom. Cut and sew 2 1/2" bias strips to make 180".
   From dark green print for second border, cut 2 pieces 3" x 39 1/2" for sides and 2 pieces 3" x 44 1/2" for top and bottom.
   From green print for backing, cut a 45" square.
3. Following Block Piecing Guide, sew 4 blocks. Sew a 12 1/2" block border strip to each side, then a 14 1/2" strip to each top and bottom.
4. Sew 84 wild goose units.

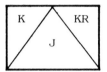

Following photograph, sew 12, 7-block units.

5. Sew 4 units as in diagram.

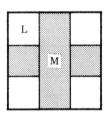

6. Sew 4 units as in diagram.

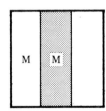

7. To make top, follow photograph to piece together units made in steps 4, 5, and 6, along with Template N.
8. From dark green solid for first border sew a 37 1/2" strip to each side, then a 39 1/2" strip to top and bottom.
9. From dark green print for second border, sew a 39 1/2" strip to each side, then a 44 1/2" strip to top and bottom.
10. Position backing, batting, and top. Pin, baste, quilt, and bind according to quilting procedure in Glossary.

Quilting Suggestion: Quilt around each tree branch, trunk, and borders.

Forest Primeval Templates

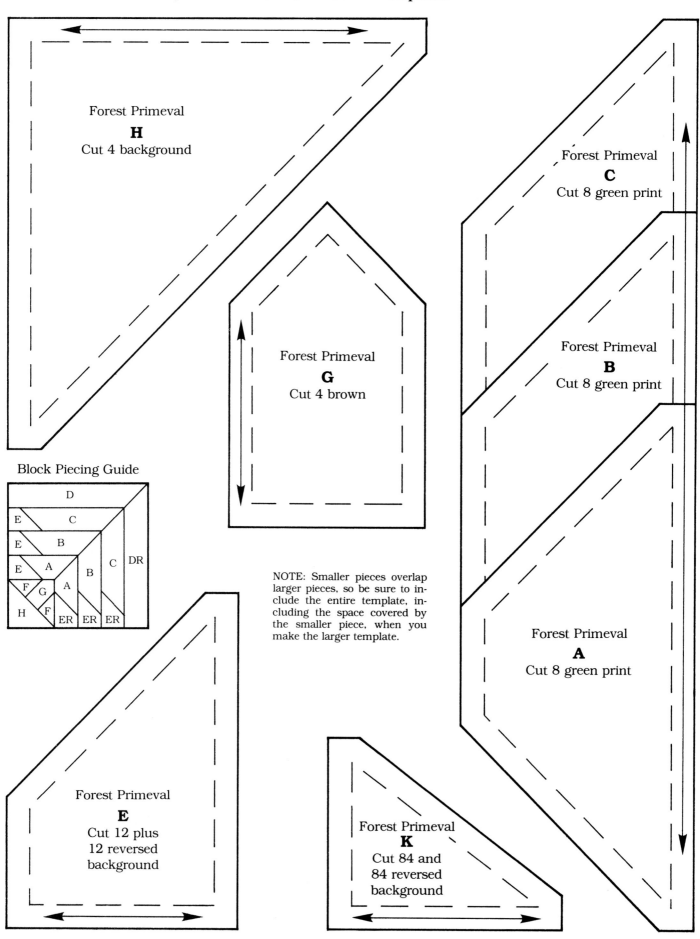

Forest Primeval
H
Cut 4 background

Forest Primeval
C
Cut 8 green print

Forest Primeval
B
Cut 8 green print

Forest Primeval
G
Cut 4 brown

Block Piecing Guide

Forest Primeval
A
Cut 8 green print

NOTE: Smaller pieces overlap larger pieces, so be sure to include the entire template, including the space covered by the smaller piece, when you make the larger template.

Forest Primeval
E
Cut 12 plus
12 reversed
background

Forest Primeval
K
Cut 84 and
84 reversed
background

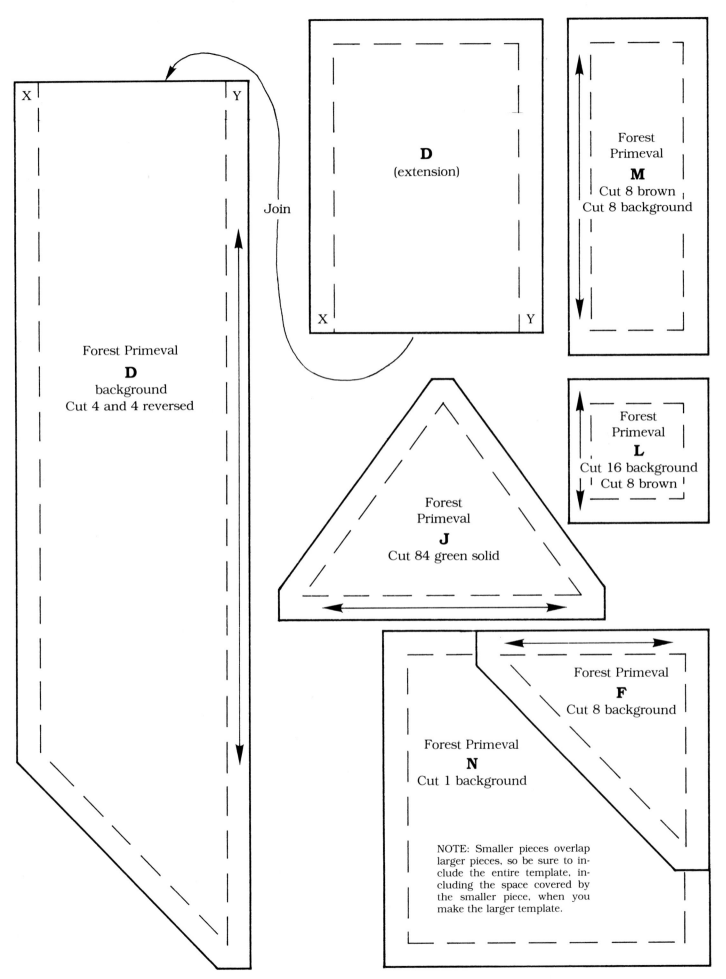

X Y

Join

D
(extension)

X Y

Forest
Primeval

M
Cut 8 brown
Cut 8 background

Forest Primeval

D
background
Cut 4 and 4 reversed

Forest
Primeval

L
Cut 16 background
Cut 8 brown

Forest
Primeval

J
Cut 84 green solid

Forest Primeval

F
Cut 8 background

Forest Primeval

N
Cut 1 background

NOTE: Smaller pieces overlap
larger pieces, so be sure to include the entire template, including the space covered by
the smaller piece, when you
make the larger template.

The Wild Goose Tree

The Wild Goose Chase is another pattern that has been popular for a long time. It lends itself to the tree motif and can produce trees as tall as space permits. Whether done as a wall hanging or a small quilt, one can become engrossed in observing movement in the blocks. Is there a goose up in the tree? See color photo on page 88.

Size: 51" x 51"
There are nine pieced blocks.

Materials:
1/4 yd. bright green print for block center
2 yds. muslin for background
3/4 yd. green print for trees
1/4 yd. brown print for trunks
1/2 yd. dark green solid for border
1/2 yd. light green solid for binding
Batting
2 1/8 yds. green print for backing

There is hope of a tree if it be cut down, that it will sprout again and that the tender shoots of it will not cease -- Job

Directions:

1. Make Templates A-F.
2. Cut from fabric as directed on templates. In addition:

From dark green solid for border make 2 strips 3 1/2" x 45 1/2" for sides and 2 strips 3 1/2" x 51 1/2" for top and bottom.

From light green solid for binding cut and sew 2 1/2" bias strips to make 200".

From light green print for backing, make a 55" square.

From batting, cut a 55" square.

3. Following Block Piecing Guide, sew 9 blocks.
4. Arrange blocks according to photograph and sew in rows, then sew rows for top.
5. Sew 1 dark green solid 45 1/2" border strip to each side, then a 51 1/2" strip to top and bottom.
6. Position backing, batting, and top. Pin, baste, quilt, and bind according to quilting procedure in Glossary.

Quilting Suggestion: Quilt around each tree and across center block. Choose a curvy pattern for the large square. See quilting pattern on page 92.

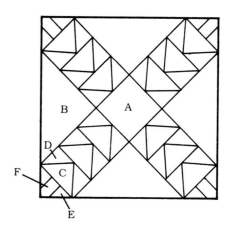

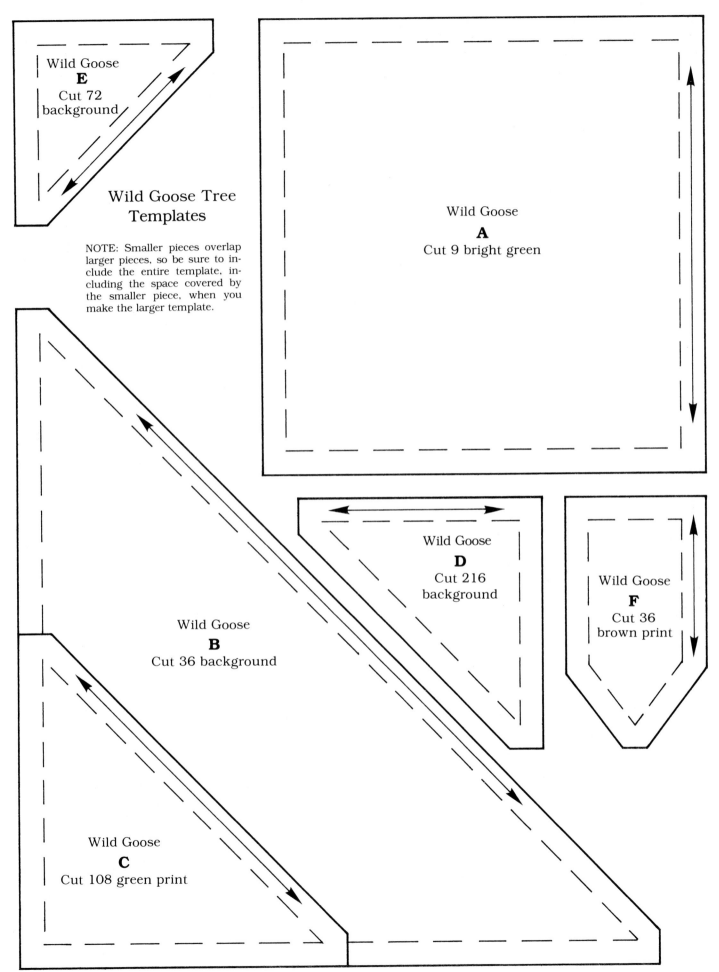

Wild Goose
E
Cut 72
background

Wild Goose Tree
Templates

NOTE: Smaller pieces overlap larger pieces, so be sure to include the entire template, including the space covered by the smaller piece, when you make the larger template.

Wild Goose
A
Cut 9 bright green

Wild Goose
B
Cut 36 background

Wild Goose
D
Cut 216
background

Wild Goose
F
Cut 36
brown print

Wild Goose
C
Cut 108 green print

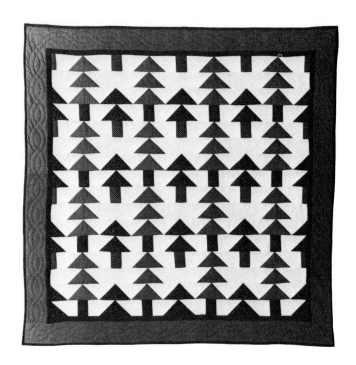

Directions:

1. Make Templates A-G.
2. Cut as directed on templates. In addition:
   From green solid for first border make 2 strips 1 1/2" x 48 1/2" for sides and 2 strips 1 1/2" x 50 1/2" for top and bottom.
   From green print for second border make 2 strips 4 1/2" x 50 1/2" for sides and 2 strips 4 1/2" x 58 1/2" for top and bottom.
3. Following photograph, sew 4 horizontal rows individually, then sew rows together to make a strip. Sew 3 other strips in same way. Join the 4 strips together for top.
4. From green solid for first border, sew a 48 1/2" strip to each side, then a 50 1/2" strip to top and bottom.
5. From green print for second border sew a 50 1/2" strip to each side, then a 58 1/2" strip to top and bottom.
6. Cut and piece green print backing to make a 62" square.
7. Cut batting to make a 62" square.
8. Position backing, batting, and top. Pin, baste, quilt, and bind according to quilting procedure in Glossary.

Quilting Suggestion: Outline quilt each tree and quilt a small design in each G piece. See design on page 93.

Forest Glorious

Block designs that form another pattern when sewn together have always intrigued me. This is such a design. It was originally drawn as a block and can still be used that way; however, the flow of the design is enhanced when sewn in strips, like the sample quilt.

This quilt is like a walk through the woods. Do you wonder what is behind each tree? Color photo on page 86.

Size: 58" x 58"

Materials:

1/2 yd. light green print for 3-branch tree
1/2 yd. dark green print for 2-branch tree
1/8 yd. brown for 3-branch tree trunk
1/8 yd. brown for 2-branch tree trunk
3/4 yd. muslin for background
1 yd. green solid for first border and binding
2/3 yd. green print for second border
1 3/4 yds. green print for backing
Batting

Row Piecing Guide

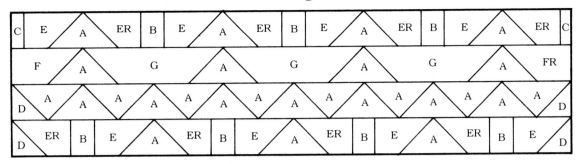

Forest Glorious Templates

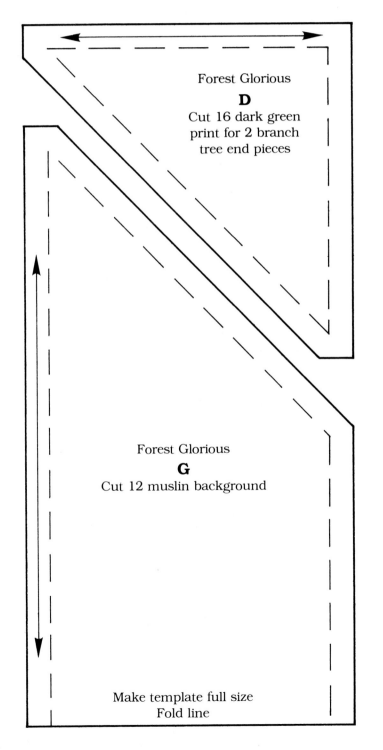

Forest Glorious
D
Cut 16 dark green
print for 2 branch
tree end pieces

Forest Glorious
G
Cut 12 muslin background

Make template full size
Fold line

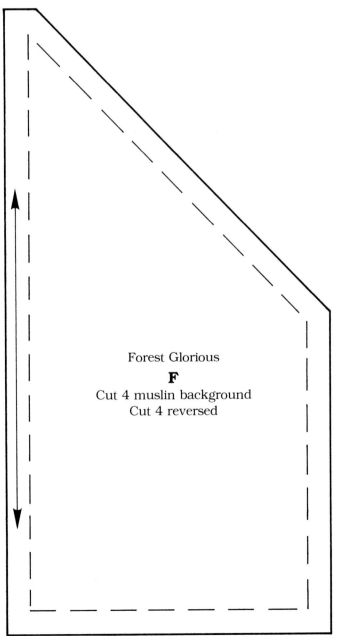

Forest Glorious
F
Cut 4 muslin background
Cut 4 reversed

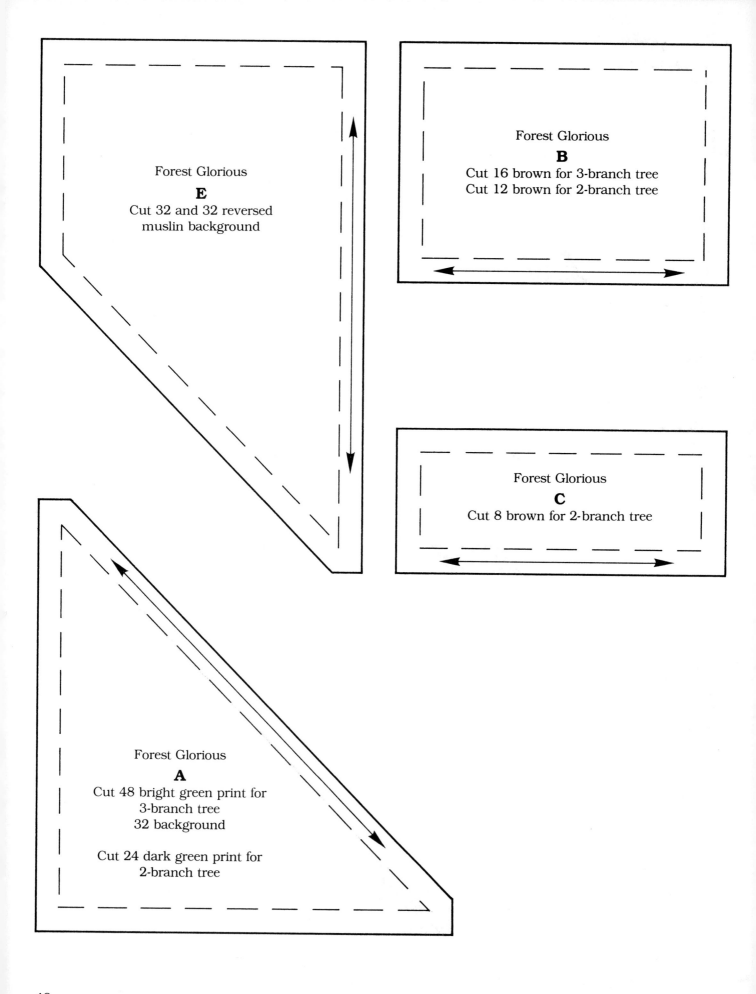

Forest Glorious
E
Cut 32 and 32 reversed
muslin background

Forest Glorious
B
Cut 16 brown for 3-branch tree
Cut 12 brown for 2-branch tree

Forest Glorious
C
Cut 8 brown for 2-branch tree

Forest Glorious
A
Cut 48 bright green print for
3-branch tree
32 background

Cut 24 dark green print for
2-branch tree

The Quickie Strippy Tree

The two words "quick quilt" have always intrigued me. They don't seem to go together, but they really do apply to this design. This tree banner is quickly put together.

The banner is made by sewing varying widths of cloth into strips, then cutting and resewing matching triangular pairs together to make square blocks, producing an overall tree design.

A full-size quilt can easily be made using this method. Try varying the widths of the strips for a different visual effect. Have fun with this design; but beware, it can be addictive! Page 15 shows this banner in color.

Size: 18" x 28"

Materials:

1/4 yd. each dark green solid, light green print, bright green solid, and medium green print
2/3 yd. muslin for backing
4 small gold tassels or ball fringe for trim
18" curtain rod

Directions:

1. Make template.
2. Cut green fabrics as follows:
   From dark green solid cut 4 pieces 1 3/4" x 44"
   From light print cut 4 pieces 1 1/4" x 44"
   From bright solid cut 4 pieces 1 3/4" x 44"
   From medium print cut 4 pieces 2 1/4" x 44"
3. Sew 4 strips in the following sequence:

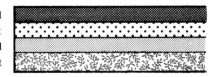

4. Fold each strip in half, wrong sides together, matching short ends.
5. Using template, cut folded strip into triangles. Keep each "pair" together. There will be 15 pairs in each configuration.

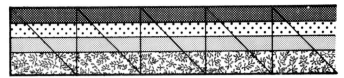

6. Sew 12 A and 10 B pairs together along longest side of triangle, carefully matching each seam. You will have 2 sets of blocks A and B.

7. Following photograph, lay out blocks alternating A and B and filling in with B half blocks on edges.
8. Sew blocks and rows together. Leave points on top and bottom rows.
9. Lay top right side down on backing, cut out and sew around all edges leaving room to turn.
10. Turn right side out and press. Add tassels to bottom and tack back top points at top for rod casing.

Quilting Suggestion: Quilt as desired, or leave as is. For a puffier banner, add batting during step 9, and quilt.

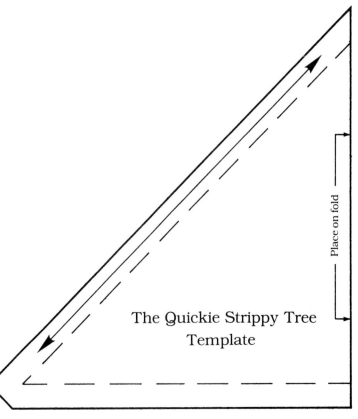

The Quickie Strippy Tree
Template

Place on fold

49

The Bear Tree

This design originated from the Bear Paw pattern and "grew" into a tree. In keeping with the original idea, a bear is quilted in each tree. Use the subtle greens of one coordinated fabric family to make the quilt. This allows for creativity in placing matching fabrics together. Add a matching stripe print for a border, being sure to miter the corners. The bears may be almost invisible, but you know they are peeking out from the branches! Page 14 shows this quilt in color.

Size: 54" x 54"

Materials:

1 yd. green print for trees and corners G
1/4 yd. brown print for trunks
1 1/2 yds. dark green solid for sashing, first border, and
　　binding
2/3 yd. light green print for paw sashing background
1 2/3 yds. light green print for block background
1/2 yd. green print for second border (1 1/2 yd. if strip
　　print is used)
1 3/4 yds. green print for backing
Batting

Directions:

1. Make Templates A-G.
2. Cut as directed on templates. In addition:
　From green solid for first border make 2 strips 1 1/2"
x 48 1/2" for sides and 2 strips 1 1/2" x 46 1/2" for top
and bottom.

From print for second border make 2 strips 3 1/2" x 54 1/2" for sides and 2 strips 3 1/2" x 48 1/2" for top and bottom. If using stripe material, add 6" to each border piece.

From green print for backing cut and sew to make a piece 58" x 58".

From dark green solid for binding, cut and sew 2 1/2" bias strip to make 230".

3. Following Block Piecing Guide, sew 9 tree blocks and 24 sashing blocks.

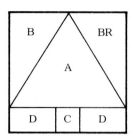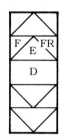

4. Following photograph, arrange tree and sashing blocks with corners G. Sew together in rows, then sew rows together for top.

5. From dark green solid for first border, sew a 48 1/2" strip to each side, then a 46 1/2" strip to top and bottom.

6. From green print for second border, sew a 54 1/2" strip to each side, then a 48 1/2" strip to top and bottom. If stripe is used, miter corners matching stripes, following directions in Glossary.

7. Position backing, batting, and top. Pin, baste, quilt, and bind according to quilting procedure in Glossary.

Quilting Suggestion: Quilt around each tree and "paw." Add a teddy bear in center of each tree or corner block.

Quilting Design from Shirley Thompson, **It's Not a Quilt Until It's Quilted** ©, *Powell Publications, P.O. Box 513, Edmonds, Washington 98020.*

50

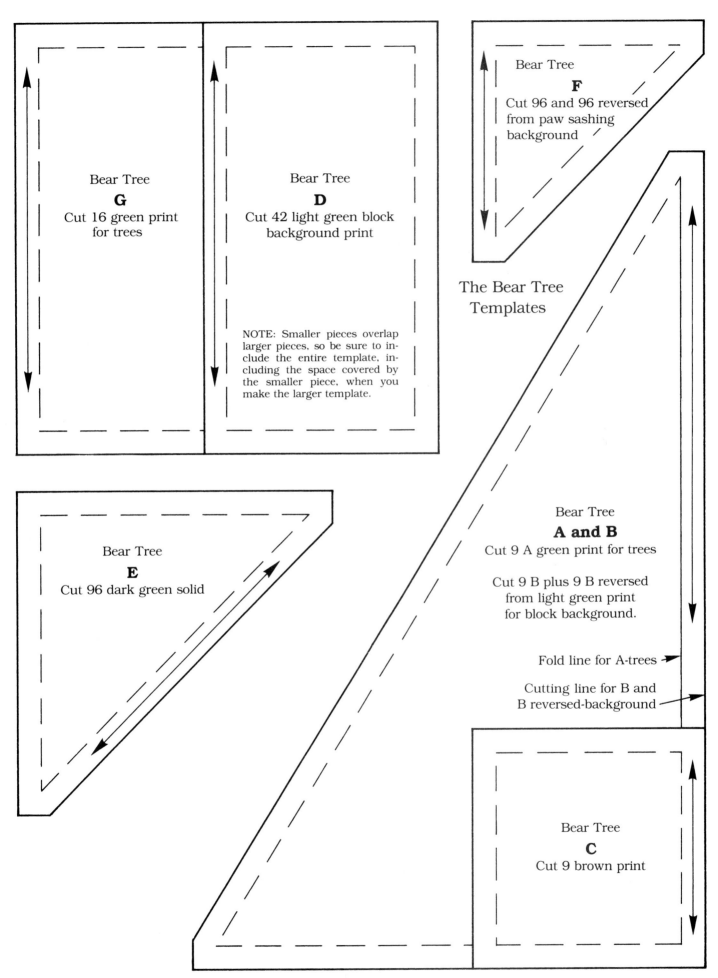

Bear Tree
G
Cut 16 green print
for trees

Bear Tree
D
Cut 42 light green block
background print

NOTE: Smaller pieces overlap
larger pieces, so be sure to include the entire template, including the space covered by
the smaller piece, when you
make the larger template.

Bear Tree
F
Cut 96 and 96 reversed
from paw sashing
background

The Bear Tree
Templates

Bear Tree
E
Cut 96 dark green solid

Bear Tree
A and B
Cut 9 A green print for trees

Cut 9 B plus 9 B reversed
from light green print
for block background.

Fold line for A-trees

Cutting line for B and
B reversed-background

Bear Tree
C
Cut 9 brown print

51

Directions:

1. Make Templates A and B.
2. Cut as directed on templates A-E. In addition:

From red-on-white background print for alternate blocks, cut 7, 8 1/2" x 18 1/2" blocks.

From red solid for border, make strips 3" x 54 1/2" for sides and 2 strips 3" x 44 1/2" for top and bottom.

From heart print for ruffle, cut 13 strips 4" x 44".

From heart print for backing make backing 48" x 62".

3. Following block piecing guide, sew 8 blocks. Applique heart to each block, following Paper Patch method in Glossary.
4. Following photograph, arrange pieced and alternate blocks and sew in rows, then sew rows for top.
5. From red solid for border, sew a 54 1/2" strip to each side, then one 44 1/2" strip to top and bottom.
6. For ruffle border, see folded ruffle directions in Glossary. Sew ruffle to top.
7. Position backing, batting, and top. Pin, baste, and quilt according to quilting procedure in Glossary.
8. To finish edge, turn under seam allowance on backing and blind stitch to ruffle base.

Quilting Suggestion: Find several heart patterns and quilt in alternate squares in contrasting color.

The Love Tree

This small quilt may be classified as a "fun" quilt. Designed to be used for a baby's crib, a child's nap, or as an adult's lap quilt, this quilt will bring a whimsical smile to those who use it. Trees have feelings, so of course they must have hearts. See page 14.

Size: 44" x 58"

Materials:

1 yd. green print for trees
1 3/4 yds. red-on-white heart print for background
1/8 yd. brown print for trunks
3/4 yd. red solid for hearts and border
1 1/2 yd. white-on-red heart print for ruffle
2 yds. heart print for backing
Batting

The pastures of the wilderness have sprung up and are green for the tree bears its fruit.
-- Joel

The Love Tree Templates

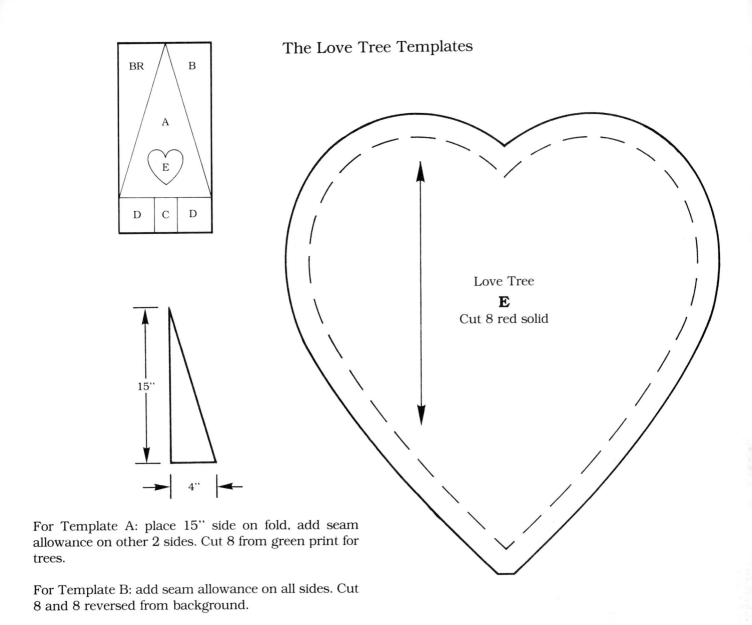

Love Tree
E
Cut 8 red solid

15"

4"

For Template A: place 15" side on fold, add seam allowance on other 2 sides. Cut 8 from green print for trees.

For Template B: add seam allowance on all sides. Cut 8 and 8 reversed from background.

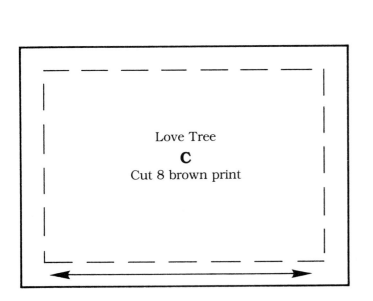

Love Tree
C
Cut 8 brown print

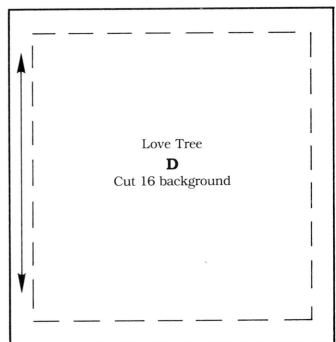

Love Tree
D
Cut 16 background

Four Seasons Dresden Tree

This wall hanging depicts the changing seasons of the year using the Dresden Tree design. See page 30. It would fit elegantly into a narrow horizontal niche. Individual blocks could be made as welcome banners for the front door and changed with the seasons. Add special touches that relate to the seasonal changes in your local area. Maybe you have lots of snow, or many evergreen trees, or only slight seasonal changes -- the sky is the limit so let your imagination run wild for a "custom" hanging. See page 82.

Size: 58" x 19"

Materials:

3/4 yd. muslin for background
4 brown scraps for trunks
4 solid scraps to match trees
4 sets of 12 scrap prints for leaves
1 yd. dark green solid for sashing and prairie points
1 yd. green print for backing
Batting

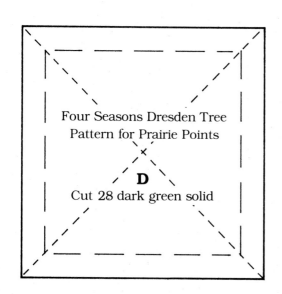

Four Seasons Dresden Tree
Pattern for Prairie Points

D

Cut 28 dark green solid

Directions:

1. Use Templates A-C from The Dresden Tree on page 31, and D from this page.
2. From muslin for background cut 4, 12 1/2" squares.
   From brown print for trunks, cut 4 A.
   From solid scraps for tree centers cut 4 C.
   From 4 sets of 12 matching prints for leaves cut 12 B from each set.
   From dark green solid for sashing strips cut 5 pieces 2 1/2" x 12 1/2" and 2 strips 2 1/2" x 58 1/2" for top and bottom.
   For hanging strips cut 5 pieces 5" x 8 1/2". For prairie points cut 28 D.
   From green print for backing, cut and sew to make a piece 16 1/2" x 58 1/2". Cut batting the same size.
3. Following Block Piecing Guide for the Dresden Tree on page 31, and Paper Patch applique instructions in Glossary, applique trunks, leaves, and centers to each block.
4. Following Quilt Piecing Guide, position and sew 5 sashing strips to blocks, then 58 1/2" strips to top and bottom.
5. Sew the long edges together on the 5 hanging strips. Turn and press. Fold D pieces on diagonal, then fold again as in diagram, and press.
6. On quilt top piece, position hanging strips at top and prairie points on bottom with raw edges even. Baste.

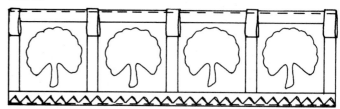

7. Position backing and batting on top, right sides together and sew around edge leaving turning opening on one side.
8. Turn right side out, press lightly and slip stitch edge. Quilt as desired.

Quilting Suggestion: Quilt birds, flowers, or animals for each season. Quilt around each leaf, trunk, and center.

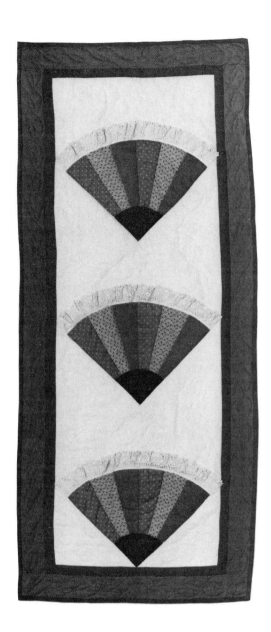

The Fan Tree

For a mind-stretching exercise, take a look at traditional quilt patterns to find trees. One of these is Grandmother's Fan. These blocks can be placed in any configuration and a new pattern will emerge. By setting the blocks on point and using greens and browns, it takes on the shape of, you guessed it, trees. Add some lace and borders and you will have a delightful wall quilt! See color photo on page 15.

Size: 24" x 57"

Materials:
7/8 yd. muslin for background
1/4 yd. or scraps of three prints for fans
1/8 yd. or scraps of brown for trunk
3/4 yd. green solid for first border and binding
1/3 yd. green print for second border
1 1/2 yds. print for backing
Batting
1 1/2 yds. gathered lace for tops of fans

Directions:

1. Make Templates A-E. Note fold and cut lines on A and B.
2. Cut as directed on templates, watching grain line. In addition:

From green solid for first border, make 2 strips 1 1/2" x 50 1/2" for sides and 2 strips 1 1/2" x 18" for top and bottom. Cut and sew 2 1/2" bias strips to make 172".

From green print for second border make 2 strips 3" x 52 1/2" for sides and 2 strips 3" x 24" for top and bottom.

From print for backing, make a piece 28" x 61".

From batting, cut a piece 28" x 61".

3. Sew 6 E to make fan. Add corner piece D, carefully sewing curved seam. Add C at top. Make 2 more blocks.
4. Following Quilt Piecing Guide, arrange 3 fan blocks and blocks A and B. Sew in diagonal rows to make rectangle 17 1/2" x 50".
5. From solid for first border, sew a 50 1/2" strip to each side, then a 18" strip to top and bottom.
6. From print for second border, sew a 52 1/2" strip to each side, then a 24" strip to top and bottom.
7. Hand sew lace to top of fan. You may need to hand tack lace to help it stand up.
8. Position backing, batting, and top. Pin, baste, quilt, and bind according to quilting procedure in Glossary.

Quilting Suggestion: Use ornate scroll designs in background blocks and quilt between each fan piece.

Quilt Piecing Guide

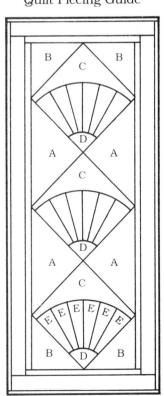

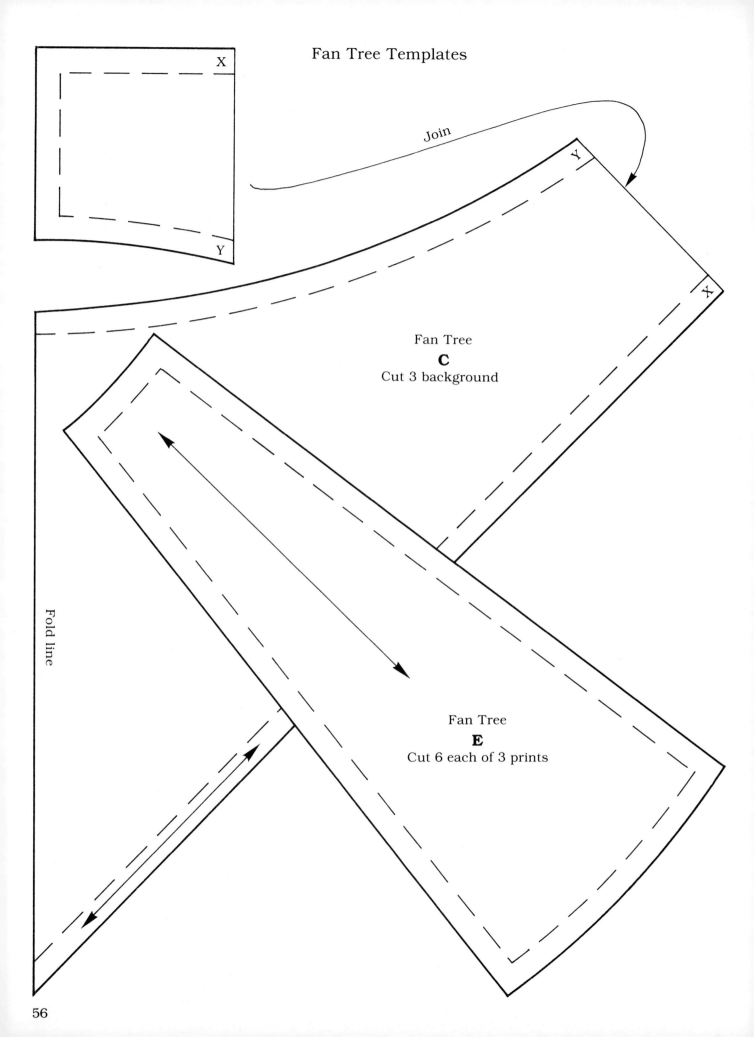

Fan Tree Templates

X

Join

Y

X

Fan Tree
C
Cut 3 background

Fold line

Fan Tree
E
Cut 6 each of 3 prints

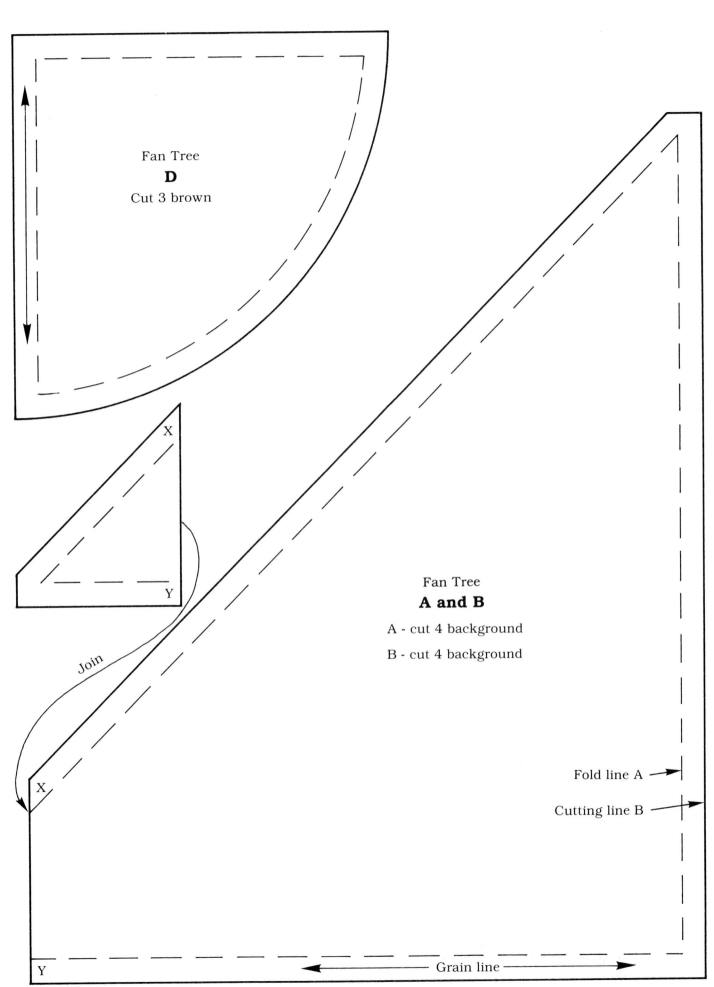

Fan Tree
D
Cut 3 brown

X

Y

Join

X

Y

Fan Tree
A and B

A - cut 4 background

B - cut 4 background

Fold line A →

Cutting line B →

← Grain line →

57

The Whimsy Tree

The rectangular blocks and autumn colors in this quilt are reminiscent of a leisurely stroll down a maple-lined street just about anywhere. A variety of colors can be found in the leaves of fall, and one look in the scrap bag produces numerous prints to incorporate into this tree quilt.

One of the fun things about this quilt is the quilting in and around the trees. A close look shows animals, birds, and leaves all quilted in response to a "whim." See color picture on page 11.

Size: 48" x 61"

Materials:
Scraps for trees as desired
1/4 yd. brown print or scraps for trunks
2 1/2 yds. muslin for background and backing
1 yd. brown solid for first border and binding
3/4 yd. rust solid for second border
Batting

Directions:

1. Make Templates A-E.
2. Cut as directed on templates. In addition:
   From muslin for backing, make a piece 52" x 62".
   Cut batting 52" x 65".
   From brown solid for first border, make 2 strips 1 1/2" x 50 1/2" for sides and 2 strips 1 1/2" x 38 1/2" for top and bottom. Cut and sew 2 1/2" bias strips to make 225".
   From rust solid for second border, make 2 strips 5" x 52 1/2" for sides and 2 strips 5" x 48 1/2" for top and bottom.
3. Following photograph, arrange scrap pieces A and B in a pleasing combination and sew in horizontal rows.
4. For rows 1, 3, and 5 sew 6 brown trunks C alternately with 5 white E, starting and ending with 2 white C.
5. For rows 2 and 4, sew 5 brown C alternately with 6 E, starting and ending with 2 D.
6. Sew 5 trunk rows to 5 matching tree rows, then sew these strips together to complete top.
7. For first border, sew a 50 1/2" brown strip to each side, then a 38 1/2" strip to top and bottom.
8. For second border, sew a 52 1/2" rust strip to each side, then a 48 1/2" strip to top and bottom.
9. Position backing, batting, and top. Pin, baste, quilt, and bind according to quilting procedure in Glossary.

Quilting Suggestion: Randomly quilt birds, animals, and leaves in and around trees. The scrap prints you use may suggest how to quilt in the design. Carefully study each print and quilt accordingly.

Quilting design from Shirley Thompson. **The Finishing Touch**©*, Powell Publications, P.O. Box 513, Edmonds, Washington 98020.*

For you shall go out with joy and be led forth in peace; the mountains shall break forth into singing and all the trees of the field shall clap their hands. -- Isaiah

58

The Whimsy Tree Templates

NOTE: Smaller pieces overlap larger pieces, so be sure to include the entire template, including the space covered by the smaller piece, when you make the larger template.

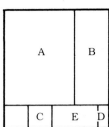

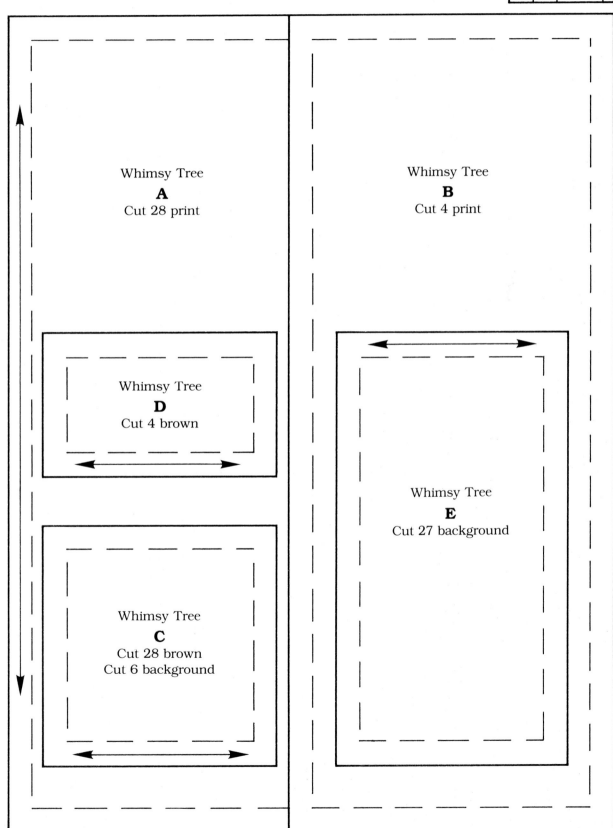

Whimsy Tree
A
Cut 28 print

Whimsy Tree
B
Cut 4 print

Whimsy Tree
D
Cut 4 brown

Whimsy Tree
E
Cut 27 background

Whimsy Tree
C
Cut 28 brown
Cut 6 background

The Christmas Star Tree

The Log Cabin has long been a friend of quilters. The turn of a block, endless color combinations, and various centers make this pattern a favorite.

This Christmas Tree has a secret hidden between its boughs. Stand back and squint -- you will see!

See this tree in color on page 12.

Size: 36" x 36"

Materials:

1/4 yd. each or scraps of 3 light, 3 medium, 3 dark prints
Brown print scraps for trunk
1/4 yd. green solid for tree border and block centers
1/8 yd. brown solid for trunk border
Batting
1 yd. Christmas print for backing

Directions:

1. From each of 3 light, medium, and dark prints for trees, cut 3 strips 1 1/2" x 44".

From green solid for tree border cut 3 pieces 1 1/2" x 44", and 9 #1 tree centers.

From brown scraps for trunk, randomly cut strips 3/4" to 1 1/2" wide.

From brown solid for trunk border cut 1 strip 1/2" x 44".

2. Using Block Piecing Guides and following numbers and prints consecutively, sew 6 blocks A and 3 blocks B as follows:

Sew #2 to #1, leaving about an inch on both ends of seam. Press then cut ends on angle of center block edge. Continue on in consecutive order.

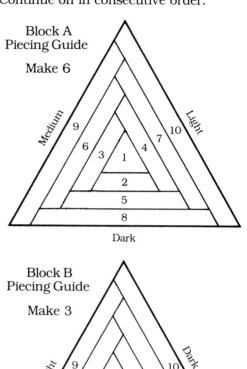

3. Join blocks following Quilt Piecing Guide.
4. Sew green solid strips to 3 sides of tree and trim ends.
5. Strip piece 2, 4" x 8" trunk pieces, using brown print strips sewn on the diagonal, to batting pieces cut to same size.
6. Sew 2 trunk pieces on 8" side. Trim to 6" x 8". Add brown solid strips to bottom, then sides of trunk piece. Position on green tree border and stitch trunk to tree.
7. Position tree and backing right sides together on batting. Pin, sew around edge, then trim to 1/4". Turn and slip stitch opening. Quilt as desired.

Quilting Suggestion: Quilt around block and centers. You may want to quilt around each log. Hang and enjoy.

Let all the trees of the wood shout for joy
-- King David

Christmas Star Tree Templates

Quilt Piecing Guide

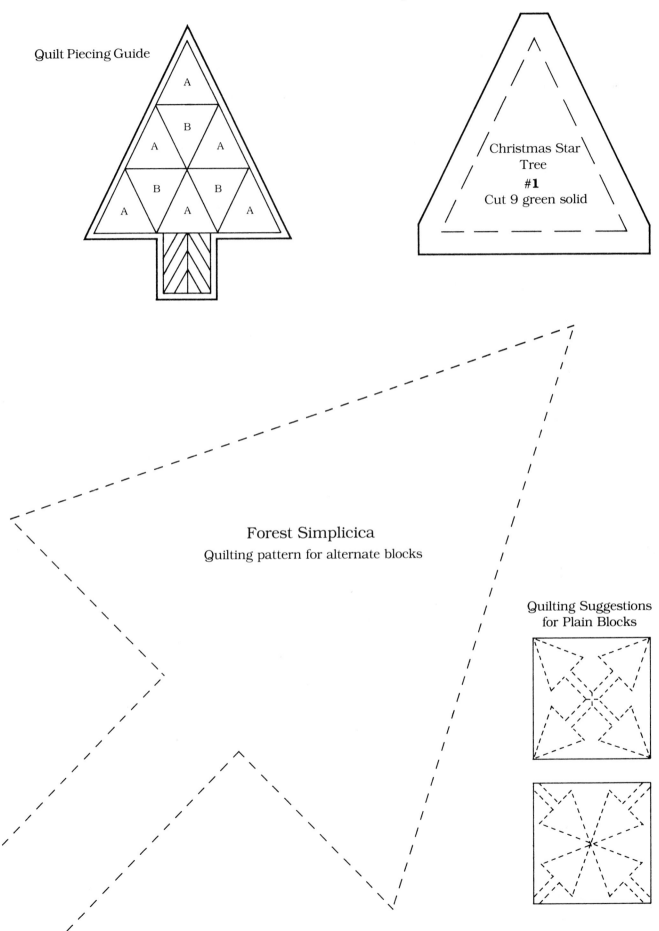

A
B
A A
B B
A A A

Christmas Star
Tree
#1
Cut 9 green solid

Forest Simplicica

Quilting pattern for alternate blocks

Quilting Suggestions
for Plain Blocks

The Cabin Tree

Schoolhouse, House, and Cabin patterns have been around for a long time. Some are tall, skinny, squatty, by a lake or on a hill, while others are just down the lane.

In thinking about designing a tall tree for a quilt, I immediately thought of a familiar, much-used place which sits in a forest of tall firs overlooking Puget Sound. Would you believe there is a cabin in this forest?

This quilt features four cabins surrounded by a forest of tall firs. A careful look in the plain alternate blocks reveals several other things that go with a cabin in the woods.

Any resemblance to a certain tall A-frame cabin on Fidalgo Island in the San Juans is *purely* coincidental!

See color photo on page 85.

Size: 65" x 78"

Materials:

2 1/2 yds. green-on-white print for background, alternate blocks, and second border
1/4 yd. each of 5 green prints for trees
2/3 yd. additional of 1 of above prints for third border
1/8 yd. brown print for trunks
1/8 yd. brick-red print for chimneys
1/4 yd. each of 4 different prints for cabins
1/8 yd. brown solid or print for doors
1/8 yd. yellow for windows
1/2 yd. dark green print for roofs
3/4 yd. dark green solid for first border and binding
4 yds. green print for backing
Batting

Directions:

1. Make Templates 1-12, A-D, and F-K. Make Template E for roof:

2. Following Block Piecing Guide for placement of prints, cut as directed on templates.

In cutting trees, cut 4 each # 1-5 from 5 different prints, then sew 1 of each print for each tree so each block will be different. In addition:

From green-on-white print for alternate blocks, cut 7 blocks 8 1/2" x 14 1/2". For second border make 2 strips 3/4" x 73 1/2" for sides and 2 strips 3/4" x 59" for top and bottom.

From dark green solid for first border, make 2 strips 1 1/2" x 70 1/2" for sides and 2 strips 1 1/2" x 58 1/2" for top and bottom.

From green print for third border, make 2 strips 3 1/2" x 73" for sides and 2 strips 3 1/2" x 65" for top and bottom. Cut and sew 2 1/2" bias strips to make 300".

From green print for backing make a piece 68" x 82".

From batting, cut a piece 68" x 82".

3. Following Block Piecing Guide, sew 20 tree blocks and 4 cabin blocks. Note that 2 cabins are reversed which calls for some rearrangement of pieces when sewing together. Be sure to cut 2 roofs reversed, position C and C reversed, A, B-K, and F-J pieces according to reverse diagram. The templates are cut as noted.

4. Following photograph, arrange and sew blocks in rows, then sew rows together for top.

5. From dark green solid for first border, sew a 70 1/2" strip to each side, then a 58 1/2" strip to top and bottom.

6. From background print for second border, sew a 72 1/2" strip to each side, then a 59" strip to top and bottom.

7. From green print for third border, sew a 73 1/2" strip to each side, then a 65" strip to top and bottom.

8. Position backing, batting, and top. Pin, baste, quilt, and bind according to quilting procedure in Glossary.

Quilting Suggestion: In block above chimney quilt puffs of smoke. In remaining plain blocks quilt a sun, moon and stars, forest animals or fish. The sample quilt shows an outhouse in 1 square, as this is significant to the cabin after which this design is made. An inspirational verse is quilted in 2" letters in the third border. It says, "For you shall go out with joy and be led forth in peace. The mountains shall break forth into singing and all the trees of the field shall clap their hands" (Isa. 55:12).

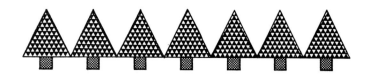

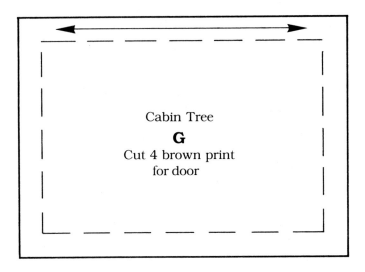

Cabin Tree

G

Cut 4 brown print
for door

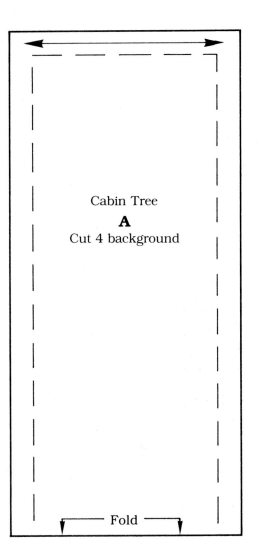

Cabin Tree

A

Cut 4 background

Fold

Cabin Tree Templates

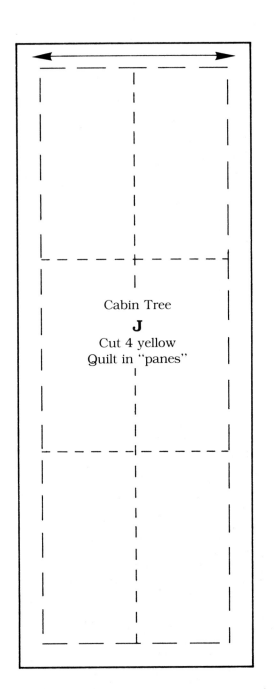

Cabin Tree

J

Cut 4 yellow
Quilt in "panes"

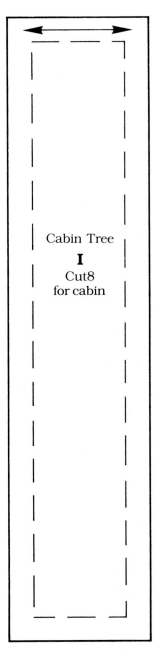

Cabin Tree

I

Cut 8
for cabin

Tree block
Make 20

8	1	8R
9	2	9R
10	3	10R
11	4	11R
12	5	12R
6	7	6

63

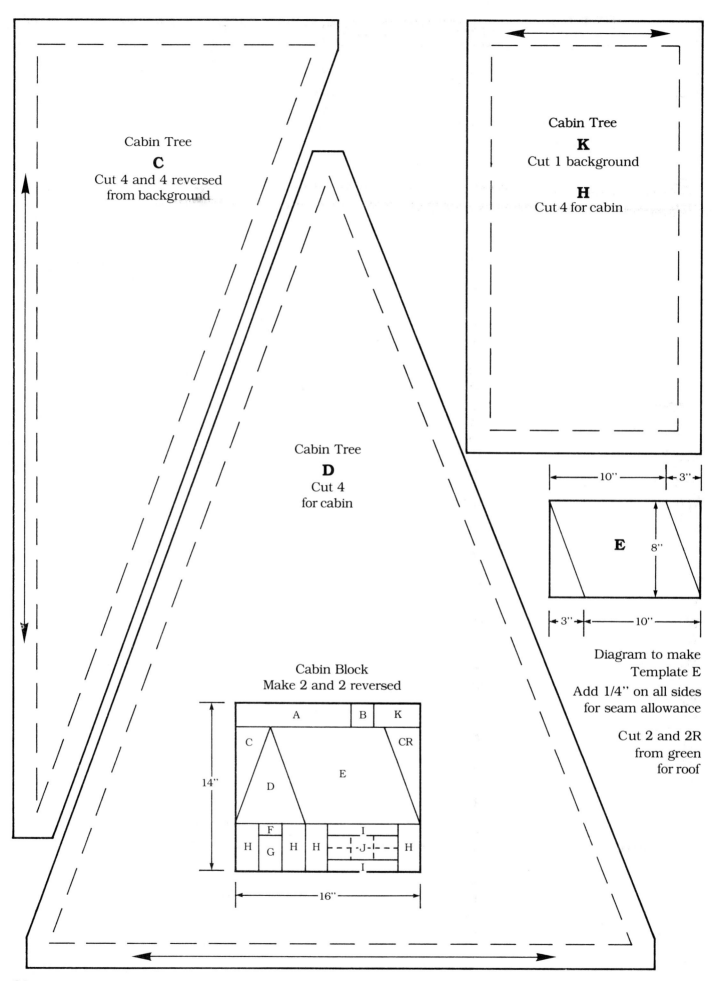

Cabin Tree

C

Cut 4 and 4 reversed
from background

Cabin Tree

K

Cut 1 background

H

Cut 4 for cabin

Cabin Tree

D

Cut 4
for cabin

10"   3"

E   8"

3"   10"

Diagram to make
Template E

Add 1/4" on all sides
for seam allowance

Cut 2 and 2R
from green
for roof

Cabin Block
Make 2 and 2 reversed

A	B	K
C		CR
	E	
D		

F
H | G | H | H | I
J
H | I | H

14"

16"

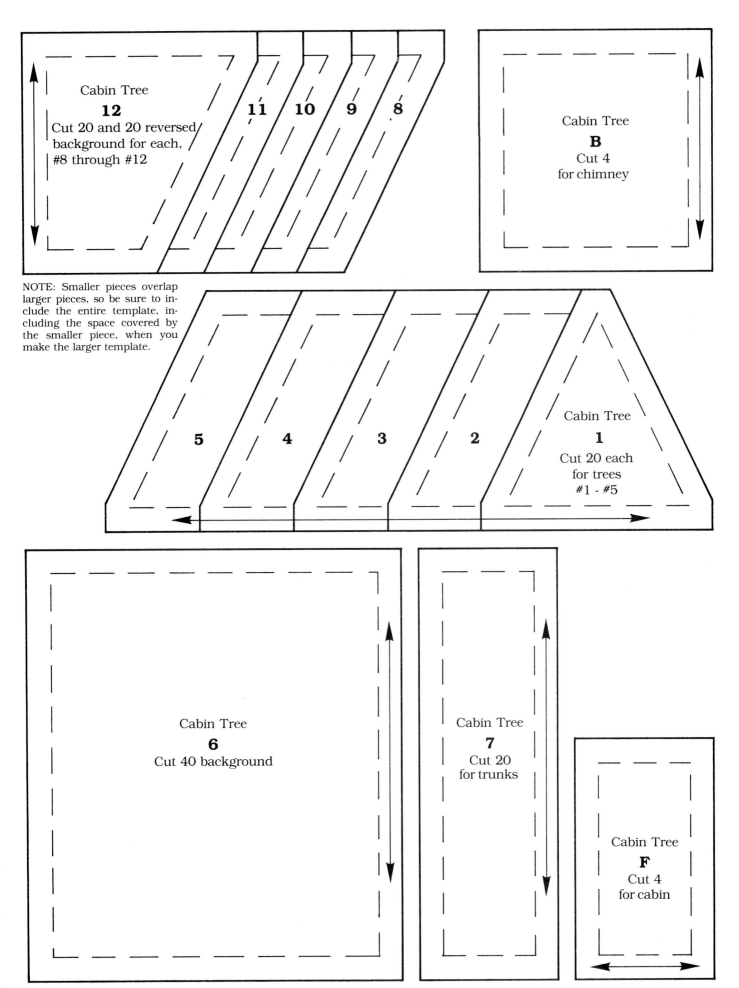

Cabin Tree
12
Cut 20 and 20 reversed background for each, #8 through #12

11 **10** **9** **8**

Cabin Tree
B
Cut 4
for chimney

NOTE: Smaller pieces overlap larger pieces, so be sure to include the entire template, including the space covered by the smaller piece, when you make the larger template.

5 **4** **3** **2**

Cabin Tree
1
Cut 20 each
for trees
#1 - #5

Cabin Tree
6
Cut 40 background

Cabin Tree
7
Cut 20
for trunks

Cabin Tree
F
Cut 4
for cabin

The Patch Tree

The nine patch is perhaps one of the oldest and simplest of all patterns. Changing the pattern just a bit and setting it on point with alternate blocks turns it into a more complicated looking pattern. Bravo! I like simplicity for its own sake, but when it can easily be made into "elegant simplicity," double bravo!! Have fun with this easily assembled tree quilt. Color photo on page 85.

Size: 33" x 41"

Materials:

1/4 yd. of 4 green prints for trees
1/4 yd. additional of 1 of above prints for third border
1/4 yd. brown print for trunks and second border
7/8 yd. green-on-white for block background and alternate blocks
1 yd. green solid for first border and binding
1 yd. green print for backing
Batting

Directions:

1. Make Templates A-E.
2. Cut fabric as directed on templates. In addition:
   From green solid for first border make 2 strips 1 1/2" x 34" for sides and 2 strips 1 1/2" x 28" for top and bottom.
   From brown print for second border make 2 strips 3/4" x 36 1/2" for sides and 2 strips 3/4" x 28 1/2" for top and bottom.
   From green print for third border make 2 strips 2 1/2" x 37" for sides and 2 strips 2 1/2" x 32 1/2" for top and bottom.
3. Following Block Piecing Guide, sew 12 tree blocks.
4. Following photograph, arrange pieced and solid blocks and sew in diagonal rows, then sew rows together for top.
5. From green solid for first border, sew a 34" strip to each side, then a 28" strip to top and bottom.
6. From brown print for second border, sew a 36 1/2" strip to each side, then a 28 1/2" strip to top and bottom.
7. From green print for third border, sew a 37" strip to each side and a 32 1/2" strip to top and bottom.
8. Position backing, batting, and top. Pin, baste, quilt, and bind according to quilting procedure in Glossary.

Quilting Suggestion: Quilt around each tree so that the trees appear to "float," and use a scroll design in each alternate block.

Quilting Design from Shirley Thompson, **It's Not a Quilt Until It's Quilted**©*, Powell Publications, P.O. Box 513, Edmonds, Washington 98020.*

The Patch Tree Templates

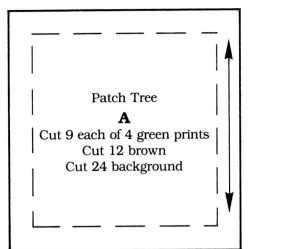

Patch Tree
A
Cut 9 each of 4 green prints
Cut 12 brown
Cut 24 background

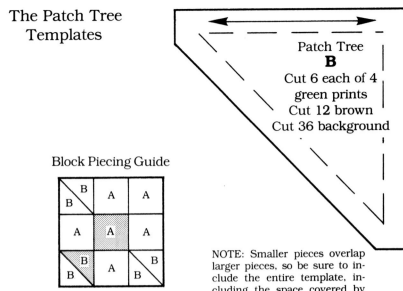

Patch Tree
B
Cut 6 each of 4
green prints
Cut 12 brown
Cut 36 background

Block Piecing Guide

B	A	A
A	A	A
B	A	B

NOTE: Smaller pieces overlap larger pieces, so be sure to include the entire template, including the space covered by the smaller piece, when you make the larger template.

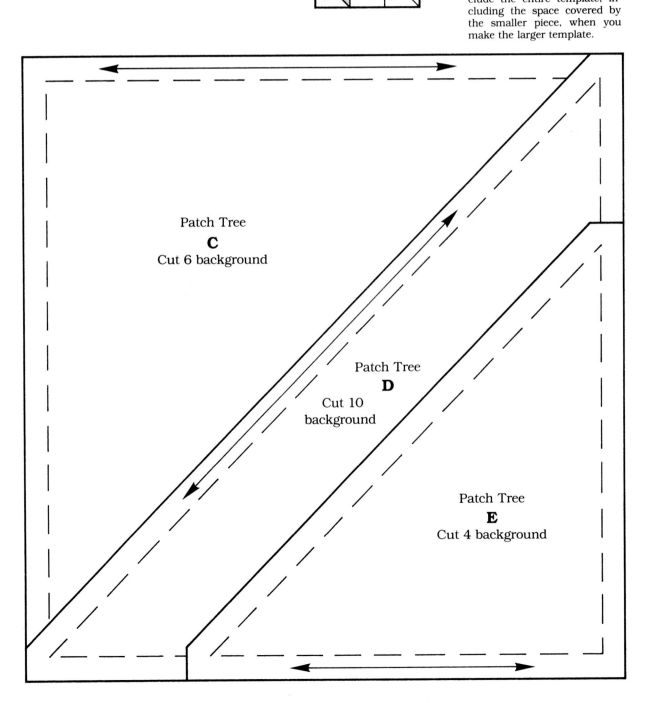

Patch Tree
C
Cut 6 background

Patch Tree
D
Cut 10
background

Patch Tree
E
Cut 4 background

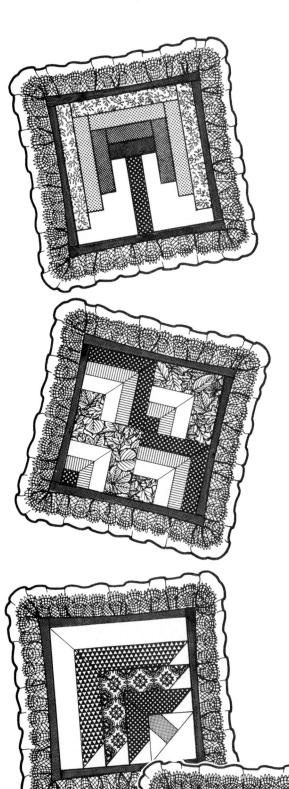

Projects

Tree Pillows

Finished size: variety of sizes

Materials:

Pillows are an excellent way to use the sample blocks you made before you made up your tree quilt; or make a pillow to experiment with a tree pattern. The amount of fabric needed depends on the pillow size. The pillow may be stuffed with a pillow form.

Directions:

1. Decide on finished pillow size. Cut out pillow back, adding 1/4" seam allowance.
2. Piece block for front.
3. Add straight sewn or mitered borders if desired.
4. Choose type of ruffle. For a folded ruffle, see Glossary on page 89. You may purchase gathered trim to add to pillow top in place of or in addition to a fabric ruffle.
5. Pin pillow back to front with right sides together.Stitch 1/4" seam, leaving an opening for turning. Turn and fill. Slip stitch opening closed.

You may choose to make a lapped back which allows a pillow form to easily slip in and out. To do this:

a.Make 2 pillow back pieces. Cut each piece the same width as pillow front. Adjust length to equal half the back length plus 2". Sew a narrow hem along 1 long edge of each pillow back piece.

b.Follow the diagram for the correct placement of the pillow pieces.

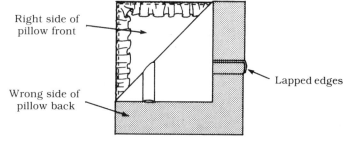

Right side of pillow front

Wrong side of pillow back

Lapped edges

c.Stitch 1/4" from all edges. Trim corners and turn to right side.
d.Insert pillow form.

Tree Pincushion

This tree's trunk holds a thimble and will come in handy when sewing. It may also be used as a Christmas tree decoration by using appropriate prints and less stuffing. The trunk would not be a thimble holder. See page 82.

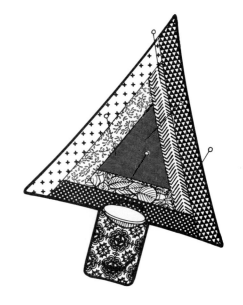

Materials:

6 green print scraps
1 brown print scrap
1 green solid scrap
Scraps of polyester fiberfil

Directions:

1. From green solid cut 1 C from Needle Case pattern, page 71.
   From print scraps cut six 1" x 6" strips.
   From brown print for thimble holder cut 2 pieces 1 3/4" x 2 1/4" and 1 piece 1 3/4" x 3 1/2". (For tree ornament cut 2 pieces 1 3/4" x 2 1/4" only.)
   From 1 green print cut 1 A from page 71 for back.

2. Sew 1 green print strip to the bottom of C, flip and press. Add strips in consecutive order to make a pieced tree. See diagram on page 70.

3. For trunk, place 1 3/4" x 2 1/4" pieces right sides together. Fold 3 1/2" piece in half crosswise, wrong sides together, and place between pieces, matching raw edges at bottom. Sew on 3 sides, leaving top edge open; turn and press. Baste raw edge to center bottom of pieced tree.

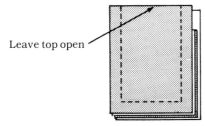

Leave top open

4. Sew top piece from step 2 to back on 2 sides, leaving bottom free. Lightly stuff. Slip stitch edges, leaving folded trunk edge free for thimble.

Needle Case

This unique needle case will find a ready place in your sewing basket. The trunk will keep your thimble in place and the pocket on the back will hold your embroidery scissors with the help of an extended trunk and two snaps. Inside is a place for your needles.

Picture on page 82.

Size: 5" x 5"

Materials:

1/4 yd. green print for inside and back
3" square green solid for pieced tree
5 other green print scraps for pieced tree
Brown scrap for trunk
1, 6" x 10" cardboard for stiffening
4 1/2" square muslin
4 1/2" square needlepunch

Directions:

1. From green print for inside and back, cut 2 A, 1 B, and 1 strip 1" x 6" for pieced tree and 3 strips 1" x 6" for inside.
    From 5 other green prints, cut 1 strip 1" x 6" for front.
    From green solid cut 1 C for front.
    From brown scrap for trunk flap cut 2 pieces 2" x 4 1/2" and 1 strip 2" x 8".
    From cardboard cut 2 A minus seam allowance.
    From muslin and needlepunch cut 1 D.

2. For pieced tree front, sew 1 green print strip to bottom of C; flip and press. Add strips in consecutive order according to diagram.

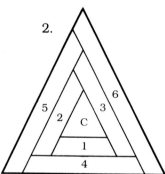

2.

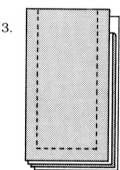

3.

3. Make trunk flap: place 2" x 4 1/2" pieces right sides together. Fold 2" x 8" piece crosswise, wrong sides together, and place between 4 1/2" pieces, matching raw edges at bottom. Sew on 3 sides, leaving top edge open: turn and press. Baste raw edges to center bottom of pieced tree.

4. Sew pieced tree front to inside (cut from A), leaving bottom edge free. Turn. Insert 1 cardboard piece and slip stitch edge.

5. Baste muslin D and needlepunch together. For inside, sew 1 print strip to each side of muslin D. Trim, using pattern piece A.

6. Fold B on line, wrong sides together, and position on right side of remaining pattern piece A. Baste in place. Stitch to inside piece (made in Direction #5) along 2 sides, right sides together, leaving bottom edge open. Turn and press.

7. Join front and back pieces along left side with whipstitch.

8. Insert scissors in back pocket and adjust trunk end so they are held tightly. Position, then sew 2 large snaps.

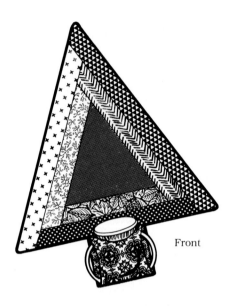

Front

Inside

Back

Needle Case Templates

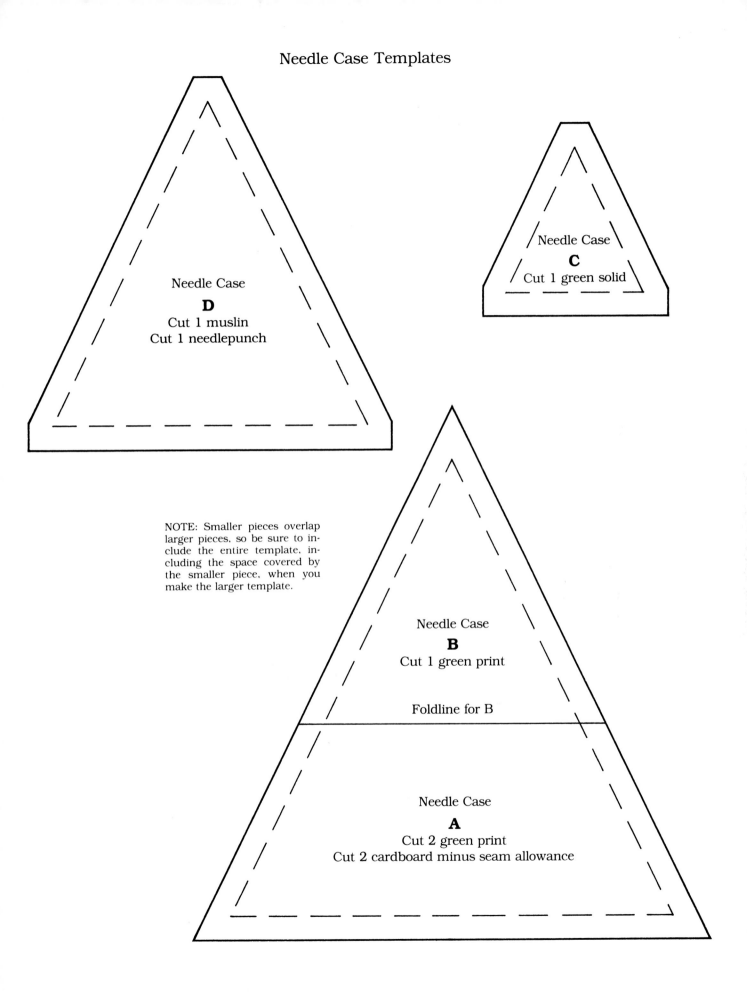

Needle Case

D

Cut 1 muslin
Cut 1 needlepunch

Needle Case

C
Cut 1 green solid

NOTE: Smaller pieces overlap larger pieces, so be sure to include the entire template, including the space covered by the smaller piece, when you make the larger template.

Needle Case

B
Cut 1 green print

Foldline for B

Needle Case

A
Cut 2 green print
Cut 2 cardboard minus seam allowance

Thread Wastebasket

This sewing aid belongs in every sewing basket or bag. It is designed to collect the thread ends that accumulate when hand sewing. It also eats the paper from paper piecing. To empty, just turn inside out and shake. Tie a ribbon on top, then make the bow around your sewing basket handle. Turn the pattern upside down and have a heart shaped thread wastebasket. Make them by the dozen for your sewing friends. Picture on page 82.

Size: 6" x 6"

Materials:

2 6" x 6" green print scraps
1 2" x 6" brown print scrap
12" double fold bias tape
1/2 yd. 1/2" gathered lace or eyelet
1 yd. 3/8" ribbon

Directions:

1. From green print cut 2 A. Cut 1 piece on tree cutting line for front. From brown print cut 2 B.
2. Bind raw edges on front with bias tape.
3. Sew 2 B pieces together leaving top open. Turn.
4. Pin to bottom of front A, raw edges even.
5. Sew lace to back A.
6. Position and pin front and back A pieces, right sides together, and sew around. Turn through bias lined slit.
7. Attach ribbon at X and tie around sewing basket handle. Note: for heart, omit B and cut front on appropriate line.

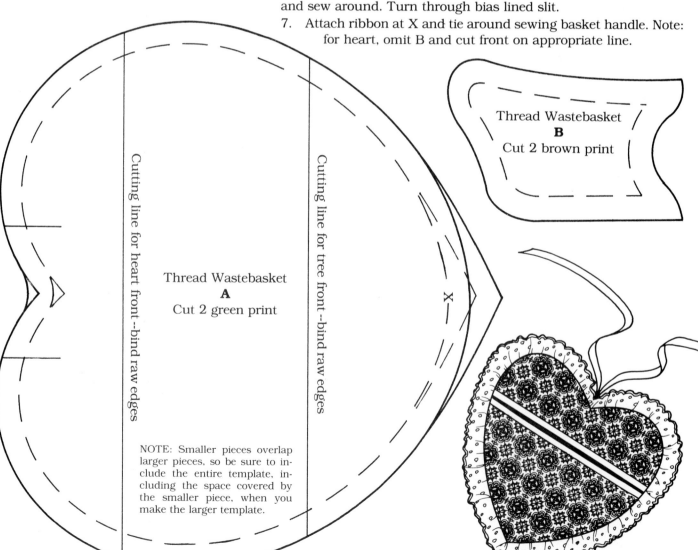

Cutting line for heart front--bind raw edges

Cutting line for tree front--bind raw edges

Thread Wastebasket
A
Cut 2 green print

Thread Wastebasket
B
Cut 2 brown print

X

NOTE: Smaller pieces overlap larger pieces, so be sure to include the entire template, including the space covered by the smaller piece, when you make the larger template.

Log Potholder

This three-sided log cabin pattern forms a nice tree to use as a hot dish mat or a potholder. It is also a thoughtful gift item.

See in color on page 81.

Materials:

1 1/2" x 9 1/2" strips of 2 different dark, medium, and light green prints
3" square of green solid
1 1/2" square of brown print
10" square of dark green print for back
10" square foil-backed needlepunch or old terry towel for filling
1 curtain ring

Directions:

1.   Using template from Christmas Star Tree on page 61, cut 1 green solid from 3" square.
2.   Following Block Piecing Guide on page 60 and arranging light, medium, and dark prints on any side you choose, sew as follows:
  Sew #2 and #1 leaving at least 1" on both ends.
  Flip and press flat, then cut ends on angle of center block edge.
  Continue adding strips in consecutive order ending with #7.
3.   Center brown print square on bottom of tree and sew, clipping 1/4" at both ends.
4.   Place right sides together with backing piece and needlepunch. Cut out, then stitch around, leaving turning place. Turn and slip stitch opening.
5.   Sew ring at top for potholder.
  Note: Use only foil-backed needlepunch as regular needlepunch will melt with heat.

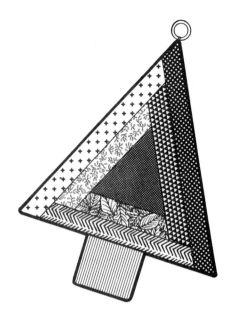

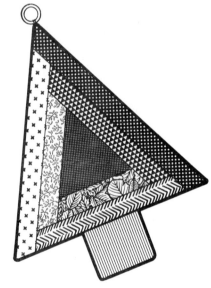

Tissue Box Cover

This tissue box cover will fit the boutique size tissues or cover a roll of toilet paper. Either way, the four trees will brighten your bedroom or bathroom. Choose a different season tree for each side and with a flip of your wrist, change your decor as the seasons come and go! Make the trees of Christmas prints and add sparkle to the holidays. The continuous pattern leaves no back seam as each row is sewn in a circle before joining rows. See page 82.

Size: 4 1/2" x 4 1/2" x 5 1/4"

Materials:
1/4 yd. muslin for background, top, and facing
Green print scraps for trees
Brown print scraps for trunks
1/8 yd. green solid for borders

Directions:
1. Cut templates. Note that G is to extend to 19" and H is to be 5 3/4" x 19".
2. From fabric, cut as directed on templates. From green solid for top binding, cut 2 bias strips 1" x 6".
3. Sew 4 green print A alternately with 4 muslin D to form a circle.
   Sew 4 green print B alternately with 4 muslin E to form a circle.
   Sew 4 brown print C alternately with 4 muslin F to form a circle.
   Sew 2 green G to make 2 circles.
4. Following illustration, sew these 5 circles to make tree, trunk, and borders.

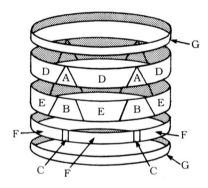

5. Sew ends of H together to make a circle. Right sides together, sew to bottom green solid border, turn and press.
6. For top, bind edge of I as indicated on template. Butt the bound edges together and baste. With right sides together pin outside edges of I top green solid border and stitch to make a square, matching slit in top with two opposite tree tops. Slip over box and pull out first tissue.

Tissue Box Cover Templates

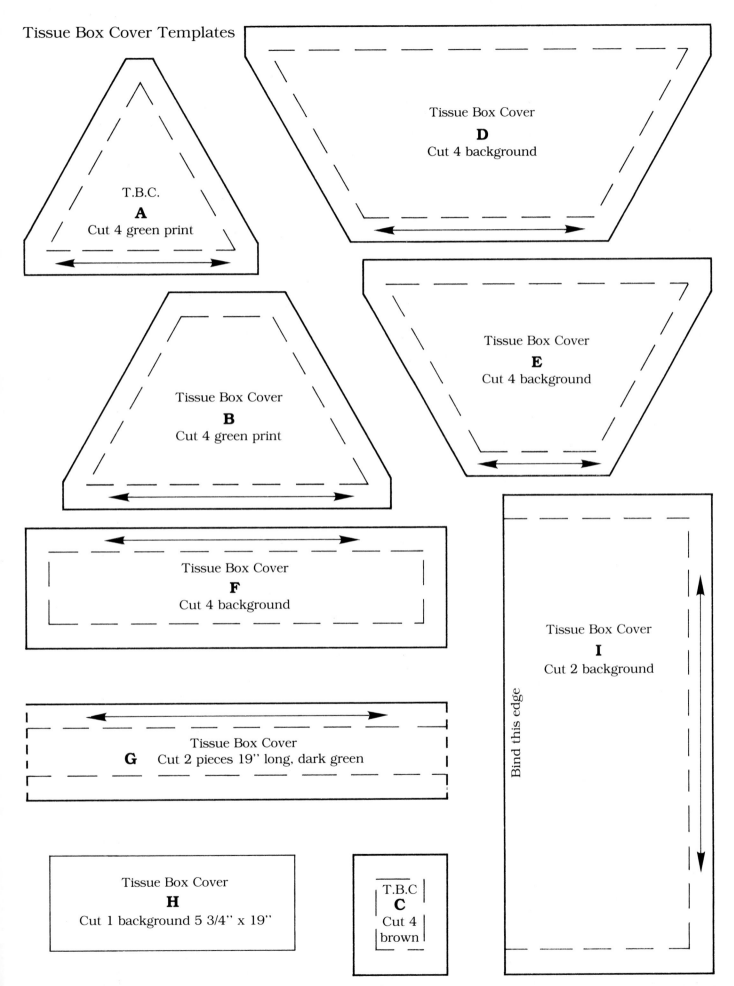

T.B.C.
A
Cut 4 green print

Tissue Box Cover
D
Cut 4 background

Tissue Box Cover
B
Cut 4 green print

Tissue Box Cover
E
Cut 4 background

Tissue Box Cover
F
Cut 4 background

Tissue Box Cover
I
Cut 2 background

Bind this edge

Tissue Box Cover
G Cut 2 pieces 19'' long, dark green

Tissue Box Cover
H
Cut 1 background 5 3/4'' x 19''

T.B.C
C
Cut 4 brown

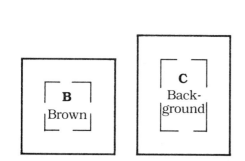

Tree Placemats

Placemats add a special touch to table settings. The addition of this simple Woodland Tree adds even more. The design is set off to one side so you can enjoy this mini forest while dining. See in color on page 81.

Size: 12" x 18"

Materials: (for 6)
2 1/2 yds. muslin for background and back
1 yd. green solid for borders and bias
1/8 yd. brown print for trunks
1/8 yd. green print for trees
1 yd. needlepunch for filling

Directions:

1. Make Templates A-D
2. From muslin cut 6 pieces 12 1/2" x 16" for front and 6 pieces 12 1/2" x 18 1/2" for back; 60 C, 30 D, and 30 D reversed.

    From green solid cut 24 pieces 1" x 2 1/2" for block sashing and 6 pieces 1" x 12 1/2" for same and 2 1/2" bias strips to make 400".

    From brown print for trunks cut 30 B
    From green print for trees cut 30 A
    From needlepunch cut 6 pieces 12 1/2" x 18 1/2"
3. Sew 30 tree blocks as follows:

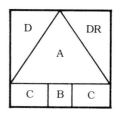

4. Using 2 1/2" block sashing pieces, sew 4 pieces between 5 blocks, making a vertical tree strip. Sew 12 1/2" sashing piece to left side of front muslin strip. Sew tree strip to this sashing strip.

5. Position back, needlepunch, and top pieces. Quilt vertical lines through all thicknesses. Trim edges to even. Bind according to directions in Glossary by sewing sides first then top and bottom. This will make nice crisp square corners.

Placemat Templates

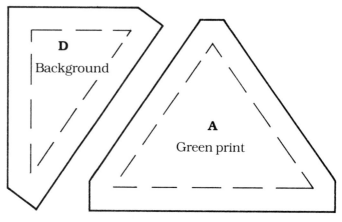

Hostess Apron

This apron adds a note of festivity to a party, or will brighten up an everyday meal. The eleven trees make a forest of enjoyment. The apron can be made with or without the bib top. The bottom muslin piece folds under to form a facing for the trees on back so no raw edges appear. You may quilt around the trees if desired. Christmas prints may be used to add to the merriment of that season or put green trees on a black background for an evening party. See page 81.

Materials:
1 1/2 yds. muslin for background and facing
Scraps of green print for trees
1/4 yd. green solid for borders
1/8 yd. scrap of brown print for trunks

Directions:
1. Cut Templates A, B, and C from Autumn Splendour quilt on page 21 and make Template D by cutting a 1 1/2" square, and Template E by cutting a piece 1 1/2" x 3 1/2".
2. Cut fabric as follows:
   Cut Muslin using diagram. From remaining muslin cut 10 A, 10 B, 10 C, and 10 E for tree panel; 4 C and 2 E for pocket; and 6 C and 2 E for bib.
   From green print for trees cut 11 A, 11 B, 10 C.
   From brown for trunks, 11 D.
   From green solid for tree panel, cut 2 pieces 1" x 36 1/2"; for pocket, cut 2 pieces 1" x 5 1/2"; for bib, cut 2 pieces 1" x 6" for top and bottom and 2 pieces 1" x 8 1/2" for sides.
3. Make tree panel by alternating pieces:
   a. sew 9 D trunk pieces to 10 E muslin
   b. sew 9 C print to 10 A muslin
   c. sew 9 B print to 10 B muslin
   d. sew 9 A print to 10 C muslin
Matching tree pieces and trunks, sew rows together and trim according to Tree Panel Diagram.
4. Sew 1 green solid strip to top and bottom of tree panel.
5. Sew muslin facing piece to bottom of green solid strip.
6. Hem short sides of apron front. Sew to top of tree panel.
7. Turn 3" of facing to apron front, right sides together. Stitch sides, then turn and slip stitch to back, forming hem.
8. For pocket, sew 1 muslin C to each side of green print A and B and 1 muslin E to each side of trunk D. Sew these rows together. Trim ends even to 5 1/2". Add green solid 5 1/2" strip to top and bottom. Place pocket piece right side down on muslin and cut out. Sew along top edge of pocket and turn. Turn under 1/4" on 3 remaining sides and top- or hand stitch to apron.
9. For ties, sew long edges together. Turn and press. Gather apron and stitch to waistband right sides together. Turn and slip stitch to back. Sew ties in waistband ends.
10. For bib, make tree as for bottom border, cutting muslin C pieces to make a piece 6" x 7 1/2". Sew a 6" green solid strip to top and bottom and an 8 1/2" strip to each side. Press and place right side down on 9" square muslin and cut out. For neck strap, press 1/4" on long sides, then fold in half and topstitch both edges. Insert strap ends at bib top corners and seam on 3 sides. Turn, attach to waistband.

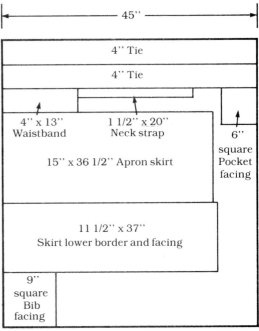

Muslin Diagram

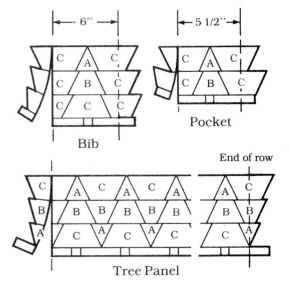

Bib

Pocket

Tree Panel

Tree Napkins

These napkins match the placemats and add a lot to the coordinated look of a table setting. The finished edge is one of the best kept secrets in sewing-dom. The seam is easy and requires no turning under narrow seams -- just use a zigzag machine and close-woven fabric. It works well on thin handerkerchief material where lace can be added as well. This project is fun however, a word of caution is in order -- the technique is addictive!

See picture on page 81.

Size: approximately 15" x 15"

Materials: (for 6)
1 1/4 yd. muslin
Green print scraps for trees
Green solid scraps for corner border
Brown print scraps for trunks
1 ball heavy green crochet thread (I prefer Speed
    Cro-Sheen)
Dark green thread

Directions:
1. Divide width of muslin into thirds. Press.
2. Fold back 1 corner diagonally to make a square.

Cut or tear on this line for 3 pieces. Measure for other 3 pieces and cut.

Using remaining muslin: cut 6 E, 6 E reversed, 6 F and 6 F reversed, 1 C.

From green solid cut 6 G, 6 D.

From brown print cut 6 B from placemat pattern on page 76.

From green print cut 6 A from placemat pattern on page 76.

3. For tree row, sew F and FR to 2 sides of A. For trunk row, sew E and ER to sides of B. Sew these 2 rows together to make tree. Sew D to bottom and G to top of tree strip. Sew C to D row.
4. Align piece with napkin corner. Place right sides together and sew to corner at top of G.
5. Flip toward corner and press.
6. Using narrow zigzag and wide stitch length, stitch crochet thread 1/4" from edge around napkin, turning sharp corners.
7. Trim seam tightly against thread.
8. Zigzag around napkin in a tight satin stitch that is wide enough to go over crochet thread. This should be just a little wider than previous stitching. Some machines have a special foot with a groove in the bottom side; this works well for this technique.

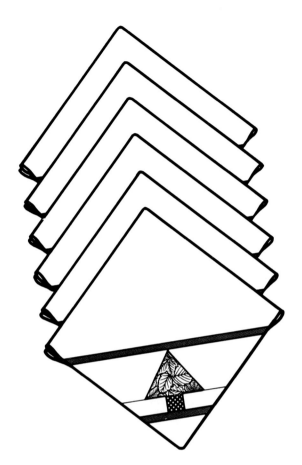

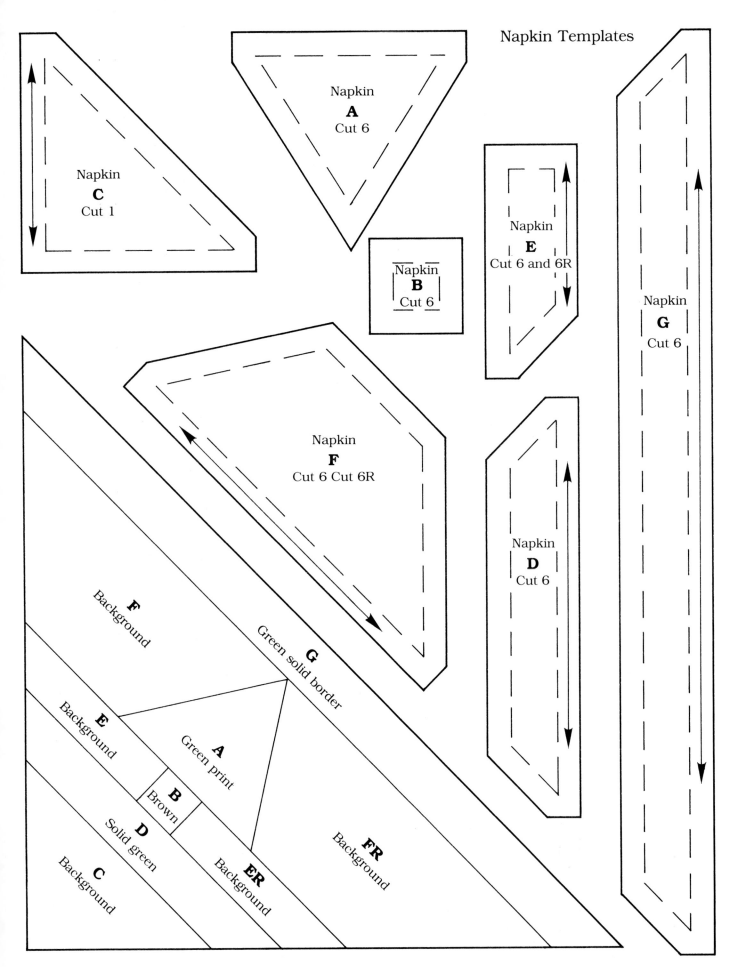

Napkin Templates

Napkin
A
Cut 6

Napkin
C
Cut 1

Napkin
B
Cut 6

Napkin
E
Cut 6 and 6R

Napkin
G
Cut 6

Napkin
F
Cut 6 Cut 6R

Napkin
D
Cut 6

F
Background

E
Background

Green solid border

G

A
Green print

B
Brown

D
Solid green

C
Background

ER
Background

FR
Background

Napkin Placement Guide

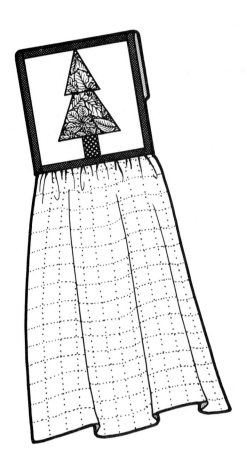

Towel Top

This kitchen accessory is a practical and decorative addition to any kitchen. It is easily made and is a nice gift item. Using Christmas prints would add sparkle to a kitchen during the holiday season. Snap one over the oven, refrigerator, or cupboard handle for easy use. See page 81.

Materials:

1/4 yd. or scrap of muslin for background and backing
Scrap of green print for tree, brown print for trunk, green solid for borders
1 kitchen hand towel (makes 2)
1 large snap
6 1/2" x 12" batting scrap

Directions:

1. Cut Templates A, B, and C from Autumn Splendour quilt on page 21 and make Template D 1 1/2" square and E 1 1/2" x 2 1/2".
2. Cut fabric as follows:
    From muslin cut 1 piece 6 1/2" x 12 1/2" for facing and 1 piece 6 1/2" square; 4 A; 2 E.
    From green print cut 1 B and 1 C.
    From brown print, cut 1 D.
    From green solid cut 2 strips 1" x 5 1/2" for top and bottom and 2 strips 1" x 6 1/2" for sides.
3. Sew 1 muslin A to each side of print A and C. Sew 1 muslin E to each side of trunk D. Sew these 3 strips together to form tree.
4. From green solid, sew a 5 1/2" strip to top and bottom and a 6 1/2" strip to each side.
5. Sew muslin 6 1/2" square to green solid top strip.
6. Position this piece right sides together on 12 1/2" muslin and batting pieces. Cut around all layers at once, making a point on the muslin piece. Start angle 3" from end.
7. Sew around 3 sides leaving bottom edge free. Turn and press.
8. Cut kitchen towel in half crosswise. Gather top to fit bottom strip of tree. Sew on bottom green solid strip, leaving facing free. Turn raw edges to inside, turn under seam allowance on facing, and slip stitch in place.
9. Sew snap on point at top and at center of bottom green strip on back side.

Celebrate the holiday with a traditional Buche de Noel (Yule Log) served on a table decorated with Tree Placemats, page 76, Tree Napkins, page 78, a Log Potholder, page 73, and a tree-trimmed Towel Top, page 80. A Hostess Apron, page 77, decorated with trees hangs in front of the Log Tree quilt.

Patchwork pillows made in various tree patterns surround a church pew, right. The Four Seasons Dresden Tree wall hanging, 19" x 58", adds a touch of color to this setting. Directions are on page 54. Trees decorate the sewing and gift ideas shown below: Thread Wastebasket, page 72, Tissue Box Cover, page 74, Needle Case, page 70, and Pin Cushion, page 69.

The Raintree quilt, 78'' x 78'', provides a variety of techniques for the quilter: The Log Cabin-like raintrees in the center, intricate quilting designs in the alternate blocks, a sawtooth pieced border around the medallion, appliqued leaves and vines, and the challenge of a ribbon border. Directions start on page 32.

Both the Alpine Tree, right, 38" x 56", and the Woodland Tree, below, 38" x 56", alternate the main block with the Puss in the Corner block. The Alpine Tree is a slender tree because of the higher elevation at which it grows, while the Woodland Tree is a squatty evergreen as shown in the blocks. Quilted by Carol Walkky and Gayle Ducey, respectively. See pages 36 and 37.

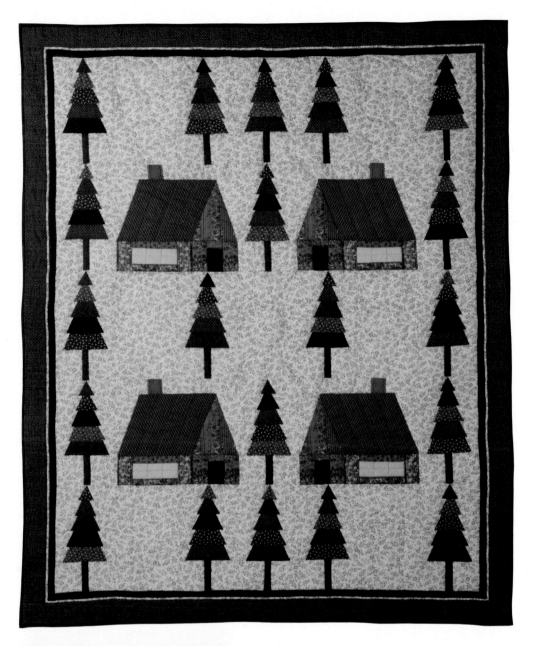

The Cabin Tree, above, 65" x 78", features four cabins surrounded by a forest of tall firs. Several suprises are quilted in the alternate blocks: sun, moon, stars, fish and an outhouse as well as an inspirational verse quilted in the border. Directions are on page 62. The Patch Tree, left, 33" x 41", is a nine patch design set on point to suggest a tree. See page 66.

The Simply Tree, above, 68" x 82", has large blocks designed for the beginner. It can be strip pieced. You can color this quilt in a warm autumn or cool spring color scheme. Page 26 has directions. Forest Glorious, right, 58" x 58", is like a walk through the woods. Do you wonder what is behind each tree? Quilted by Carolee Hammer. See page 46.

The Dresden Tree, 84'' x 84'', is based on the traditional Dresden Plate block which makes a nice crown for this tree. The twelve segments of the tree are machine sewn, then appliqued to the background with the trunk and center circle. See page 30 for directions.

The Wild Goose Tree, right, 51'' x 51'', is based on the Wild Goose Chase pattern. It lends itself to the tree motif and can produce trees as tall as space permits. Quilted by Jan Coté. Directions are on page 44. Forest Simplicica, below, 78'' x 78'', alternates thirteen pieced blocks with twelve solid blocks to make a unique quilt which will add life to any setting. See page 24.

Glossary

Paper Patch Applique

Applique is used on several of the quilts and projects in this book. You may applique by hand or machine. I prefer using a technique called Paper Patch Applique.

1. Make templates for all pattern pieces from medium weight bond paper. Do not add seam allowance.
2. Place templates on fabric. Cut 1/4" from all edges of template.
3. Pin fabric to template.
4. Fold 1/4" seam allowances over template. Baste fabric to template, using a running stitch and sewing through the paper.
5. Clip inner curves and indentations, gently stretching fabric.
6. On outer curves, ease in fullness, using a small running stitch to gather the fabric. Do not sew through paper on outer curves.
7. The basting stitches that go through the paper on either end of the outer curve will hold the fabric to the paper.
8. Baste all fabric pieces to paper. Do not use a knot after the last basting stitches since the basting stitches and paper must be removed in a later step.
9. Press all fabric pieces, easing fabric to ensure that bumpy edges are not created during pressing.
10. Applique fabric pieces to background, using a small blind stitch and matching thread. Stitches should be fairly close together. When applique of each piece is almost complete, pull basting thread from fabric and remove paper from the small opening that remains. A pair of tweezers is helpful for this step. Cut away background fabric under applique piece, leaving 1/4" seam allowance. This leaves one less fabric layer to quilt.

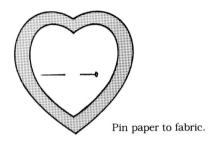

Pin paper to fabric.

Baste fabric to paper, sewing through paper.

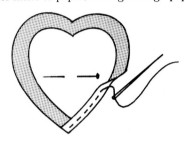

Ease in fullness on curves with small running stitch.

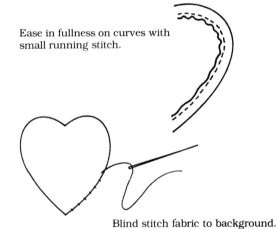

Blind stitch fabric to background.

Ruffle

1. Making fabric ruffles is easy to do and adds a nice finish to pillows or quilts. You can make a folded or hemmed ruffle.
2. Figure the length of the ruffle to equal twice the length of the area to which it will be sewn.
3. Select the width of the finished ruffle. If making a folded ruffle, measure twice the finished width, plus 1/4" for seam allowances. For a hemmed ruffle, measure the width, plus 1" for the hemmed edge and the seam allowance.
4. After determining the length and width of the ruffle, cut a strip (or strips) of fabric to equal those measurements. Seam the strips together to make a ruffle the required length.
5. To make a folded ruffle, fold the ruffle lengthwise with the wrong sides of the fabric together and steam press the length of the ruffle. Sew a gathering stitch along the raw edges of the ruffle. Gather that edge to the required length.

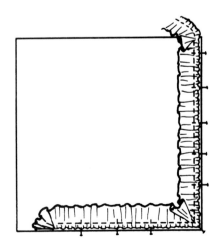

6. To make a hemmed ruffle, press one edge of the ruffle under and machine hem. Sew a gathering stitch along the remaining raw edge of the ruffle. Gather that edge to the required length.

7. Gathered trims and ruffles are attached in the same way. With the right side of the trim or ruffle facing the right side of the pillow front, pin in place with the raw edges even and the finished edge of trim or ruffle should be eased into the corners, and outer edges should be carefully pinned so they will not be caught in the stitching.

8. Take time to hide the beginning and end of the trim or ruffle. Do not start at the corners of a square piece; instead, overlap along a straight edge.

9. Adjust the gathers to fit and baste the trim or ruffle in place. If using two different sized ruffles, baste the narrower one in place first.

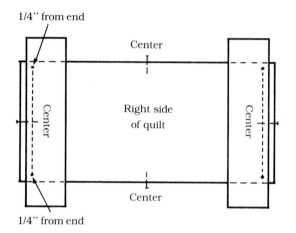

1/4'' from end

Center

Center

Right side
of quilt

Center

Center

1/4'' from end

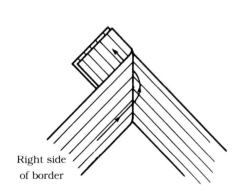

Right side
of border

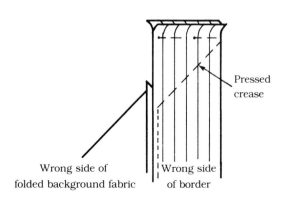

Pressed
crease

Wrong side of
folded background fabric

Wrong side
of border

Ensuring a Good Ending

Borders

The borders in this book are sewn with straight corners except for the Bear Tree, which has mitered corners. If you wish to have mitered corners, or if you are using a striped fabric, use the following instructions and diagrams.

Mitered Borders

1. Mark the center edges of the borders and quilt by folding them in half and inserting a pin at the fold.

2. With right sides together, match borders according to diagrams. Pin in place at beginning and end of seamline. Be sure to match center pins.

3. Baste and stitch two opposite borders in place, beginning and ending seams 1/4'' from ends.

4. Press seams flat with seam allowances toward the borders.

5. Repeat with remaining two borders. (Seams will begin and end at the end of the two previously stitched border seams.) Anchor these points with a pin.

6. Working on one corner at a time, fold top border under to form a mitered corner.

7. Fold borders with right sides together. Open seams and fold away from border. Insert pins through border. Check underneath to see if pins are aligned with stripes and adjust pins if necessary.

8. Baste pressed crease. Stitch on basting, outward to border edges. Remove basting. Trim 1/4'' away from seam.

Quilting Procedure

Position backing, batting and top:

Tape the backing piece to floor or table, wrong side up. Lay batting piece on top and smooth out. Carefully place top right side up over batting, making sure the batting and backing extend beyond the top several inches. Smooth out with hands.

To determine size of quilt batting needed, add 4" to length and 4" to width measurement of quilt top. This gives a generous allowance on all four sides of the quilt.

Pin:

Starting at center of quilt, pin all 3 layers together. Continue pinning at 8" to 10" intervals to edge as in diagram.

Baste:

Baste, starting at center and working out, in a 4" grid over quilt.

Quilt:

You are now ready to put the quilt in a quilting hoop or on a quilt frame. Start at quilt center and quilt out to the edges, moving hoop or turning frame as needed. Take tiny running stitches using quilting thread and needle. Check back of quilt frequently to be sure the needle goes all the way through the batting and backing.

My personal preference for quilting is to use an old-fashioned quilt frame where the quilt is put on flat, stretched taut, and rolled from both ends when quilted. This kind of frame is made from 4, 1 x 4's. Tack a narrow cloth strip to 1 long side of each board and use C-clamps in the 4 corners. Pin backing to each of 2 end pieces; stretch out, and use other pieces for sides: clamp taut. Place frame on the backs of 4 chairs. Pin backing to side pieces. Make sure the 4 corners are square and backing is taut without ripples. Roll out batting on top. Carefully place pieced top on batting. Stretch and pin at edges as necessary. Quilt from each end in as far as comfortable, about 12", then release clamps, turn end piece under, clamp and quilt another strip across until center is reached from both ends. Unwind and remove from frame.

This method eliminates basting and ensures a pucker-free back; however, space is needed to set it up and it is not portable.

Bind:

To find the true bias, bring 1 corner of fabric up to opposite corner and press. Cut on press line. Measure and cut 2 1/2" bias strips on this line. Seam ends to make 1 long strip. Fold, matching raw edges. Press. Align raw edges on bias with raw edges of quilt top edge and stitch, taking 1/4" seam. Start at 1 corner of quilt and sew to next corner, cut fabric and thread. Reposition and sew down next side. Continue around quilt. Turn under and hand stitch to back on bias fold line.

Setting up to quilt

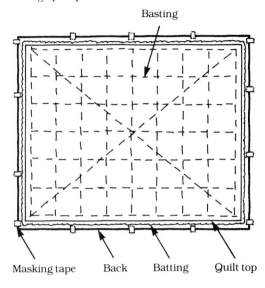

Masking tape   Back   Batting   Quilt top

Marking bias strips

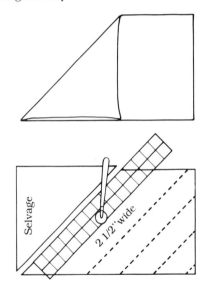

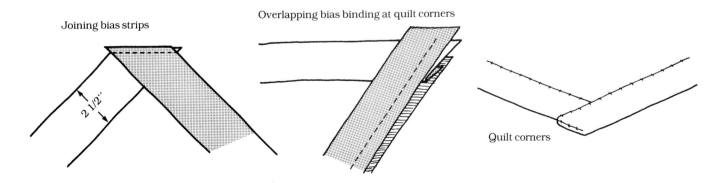

Joining bias strips

Overlapping bias binding at quilt corners

Quilt corners

91

Marking Quilting Designs

There are several ways to mark a quilting design on the quilt top. When the quilt has alternate plain blocks as in the Raintree or Forest Simplicica, it is helpful and more accurate to mark the design before the blocks are sewn together. This is easiest done by using a light table or making your own by separating a table top and putting a piece of glass over the space where the table leaf goes. Put a lamp under the glass. Tape the design, then the quilt block to the top of the glass, turn on the light and trace the sharp color pattern.

Another way is to mark the top after the top is sewn together and before positioning the batting and backing. This works well for marking borders. Use a light table and move the top as needed to mark pattern. The Fan Tree was marked this way. The Simply Tree was marked on a table top using a ruler, as the lines are simple and straight.

Because I use an old fashioned full frame, (see page 91), many times I will mark after the entire quilt is on the frame. This is possible because all pieces are taut and the entire quilt can be seen at once. The 2" grid on Autumn Glory was done like this.

If quilting in a hoop or on a rolling frame, sometimes it is more convenient to mark as needed in small areas. The pen whose lines automatically disappear after 24 hours is well used at this time. This is also the place to use the 1/4" masking tape for straight lines. Washington Splendour was marked this way on a full frame and the main part of the Log Tree on a hoop was done like this.

Examine your quilt top to see which method of marking is easiest for the design you have chosen. You might want to try something different. One nice thing about the art of quilting is that there is generally more than one way to do each step, which leaves the door open for experimenting.

Quilting pattern for Wild Goose Chase

Quilting pattern for Forest Glorious

Quilting pattern for Raintree

Quilting designs from Shirley Thompson. **The Finishing Touch**©**,** *Powell Publications, P.O. Box 513, Edmonds, Washington 98020.*

93

Labels:

When your quilt is finished, make a label for the back which gives the name of the quilt, person who made and quilted it, date completed, owner of quilt, and city and state where made. Include any other pertinent information, such as a specific occasion, special fabrics, etc. These labels can be made by typing on muslin and sewing them on, by embroidery, or cross stitch embroidery.

There are many ways of making a quilt. No one way is necessarily "correct." Some methods may be easier, look better, or take less time. Experiment with new ideas till you find one that is just right for you. Above all, enjoy what you are doing and be proud of it.

Happy Quilting!

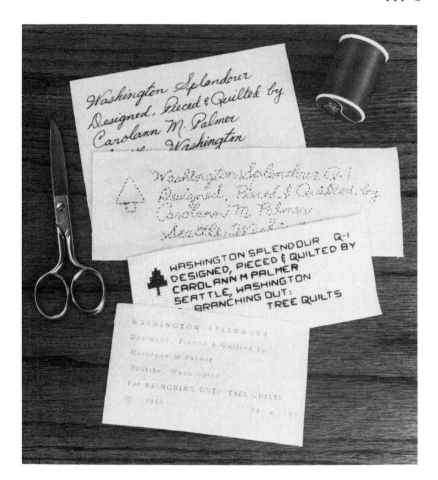

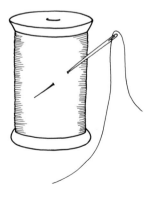

For you shall go out with joy and be led forth in peace; the mountains shall break forth into singing and all the trees of the field shall clap their hands. -Isaiah

Meet the Author

Carolann Palmer, quilt teacher and designer, is an enthused and excited quilter who is eager to share her ideas with others. Carolann made her first quilt over 30 years ago and has since made almost a hundred; 60 of these were baby quilts for friends and family. She has sewn everything from baby clothes and crib quilts to wedding dresses for her grown daughters.

Carolann receives much satisfaction from sharing her quilting skills and enthusiam. She is an active member of her quilt guild, Quilter's Anonymous, of which she is a past president. Carolann is active in church activities and likes to cook, camp, and enjoy the outdoors of the Pacific Northwest.

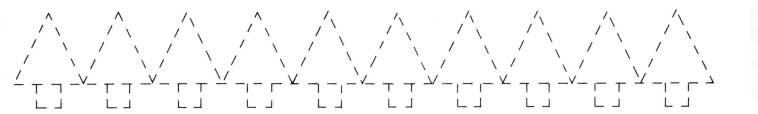

That Patchwork Place Publications

Barnyard Beauties by Mary Ann Farmer $4.00

Basics of Quilted Clothing by Nancy Martin 8.00

Bearwear by Nancy J. Martin 7.95

Cathedral Window - A New View by Mary Ryder Kline 6.00

Christmas Classics by Sue Saltkill 6.95

Christmas Quilts by Marsha McCloskey 11.95

Country Christmas by Sue Saltkill 6.00

Fabriscapes™ by Gail Johnson 5.00

Feathered Star Sampler by Marsha McCloskey 3.95

Housing Projects by Nancy J. Martin 9.95

Linens and Old Lace by Nancy Martin and Sue Saltkill 9.95

Make a Medallion by Kathy Cook 11.95

Pieces of the Past by Nancy J. Martin (June 1986) 16.95

Pilots, Partners & Pals by Mary Ann Farmer 4.00

Projects for Blocks and Borders by Marsha McCloskey 11.95

Quilter's Christmas by Nancyann Twelker 8.00

Sew Special by Susan A. Grosskopf 6.00

Small Quilts by Marsha McCloskey 6.00

Special Santas by Mary Ann Farmer 4.00

Stencil Patch by Nancy Martin 6.00

Template-Free Quiltmaking by Trudie Hughes 11.95

Touch of Fragrance by Marine Bumbalough 5.95

Wall Quilts by Marsha McCloskey 8.00

Warmest Witches to You by Mary Ann Farmer 4.00

Christmas Cards 4.95

Note Cards 3.50

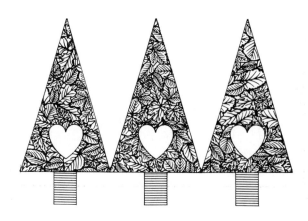

Printed in the United States of America